Women and Credit in
Pre-Industrial and Developing Societies

Women and Credit in Pre-Industrial and Developing Societies

William Chester Jordan

University of Pennsylvania Press

Philadelphia

Cover: Women, including a nun, entering an Italian pawnbroker's establishment. British Library, Add. 27695 (fourteenth century), fol. 8. Reproduced by permission of the British Library.

Copyright © 1993 by the University of Pennsylvania Press
All rights reserved
Printed in the United States of America

Library of Congress Cataloging-in-Publication Data

Jordan, William C., 1948–
    Women and credit in pre-industrial and developing societies /
William Chester Jordan.
        p.   cm.
    Includes bibliographical references and index.
    ISBN 0-8122-3194-5
        1. Consumer credit—History.   2. Women—Finance, Personal—History.
3. Women—History—Middle Ages, 500–1500.   4. Europe—Economic Conditions—
16th century.   5. Developing countries—Economic conditions.   I. Title.
HG3755.J588   1992
332.7'43—dc20   92-42835
                                                                                    CIP

FOR ELLEN MARIE

Contents

Introduction: The Parameters of the Study

My intention in this book is to synthesize much of the work done in the past several decades on women and their relation to credit in the period before industrialization.[1] The effort began with the hypothesis—indeed, the conviction—that there is something distinctive and significant about women's roles in credit. The testing of the hypothesis depended on a systematic exploration of the data on pawnbroking, investment, markets, formal credit institutions, and the like. Even at first glance, however, credit seemed to be an arena where women in the pre-modern world played a peculiar and fascinating part in the economy, for moneylending stands in sharp contrast to a characteristic feature of traditional economic arrangements, namely, the close correlation between types of work, whether paid or unpaid, and the sex of the worker.[2]

It is true that certain variables, like the level of pay and the complexity of the work undertaken, as well as change over time in these variables can have a decisive effect on the composition of the labor force, but even over the long term these factors have rarely (and then only temporarily) obliterated the sexual division of labor. To take one example, the labor force in cloth manufacture was almost exclusively female in Antiquity and through the High Middle Ages in the West.[3] A cluster of influences in the later Middle Ages first destroyed that monopoly and then recreated it for males.[4] To take another example, one where change over time is not at issue, household baking (non-remunerated) was a woman's job in the Middle Ages. In many regions, contemporary baking for the market was customarily (but not exclusively) a man's. Sometimes, of course, marketing a product did not undermine women's preponderant role in production or even impede them from vending the product of their work: whether producing for home consumption or the market, poultry raising was largely—though, again, not solely—a female preserve in the European Middle Ages.[5]

The sexual division of labor was, then, characteristic of pre-modern European society—characteristic, but not universal. Where agricultural labor is concerned, a significant long term exception occurred in low-paid drudgery; for such work men and women competed on more or less equal terms.[6] Intermittent exceptions, also of some significance, have occurred during periods of acute labor shortages, such as that following the Black Death in the mid-fourteenth century: a few tasks (reaping by sickle, the binding of sheaves, carting) customarily reserved for men underwent a somewhat "egalitarian" redistribution and, equally important, a softening of the differential between male and female rates of pay, which typically favored men over women even when the tasks performed were similar.[7]

In the service sector of the medieval economy the rigid distinctions suggested above (the anomalies notwithstanding) found parallels but also a few remarkable contradictions. Men largely monopolized public office. The priesthood was male. Professional scribes, with the exception perhaps of a few in convent scriptoria, were male. Yet men and women ran hostels, and men or women could keep taverns, although the balance of these mixed-sex occupations often changed dramatically from generation to generation.[8] Most important for the purposes of this study is that both men and women were pawnbrokers and moneylenders. The meaningful distinction within such mixed-sex occupations—besides secular changes in the ratio of men to women—concerns the nature of the services provided. Medical practitioners in time past were also of both sexes, but those who specialized in academic medicine were males and those who helped deliver babies were, until the eighteenth century, almost exclusively females.[9]

In the case before us, therefore, an important question is whether the sorts of transactions handled or clientele served by female moneylenders and pawnbrokers diverged from those handled or served by men. Another is whether the types of investments made by women differed from those made by men or institutions. Still another concerns the ban on usury and its enforcement or relaxation for that "tearful orchestra," as Tawney called it, of widows and orphans for whom ideologues pleaded, under different circumstances, both for and against the ban.[10] These and similar questions recur in the course of the book. That our focus is a sexually mixed rather than sexually exclusive set of occupations in the service sector suggests that the conclusions might modify the dominant scholarly assessment of the relative power and influence of women in pre-modern economic life, which until now has been based on the study of their contribution to agricultural labor and craftwork. The recent survey by the late David Herlihy (1990) does not address credit; yet a consideration of this kind of work is crucial in assessing the larger claim of that survey that the late

Middle Ages saw an overall decline or subordination of female participation in the economy.[11]

Interesting as the effort to synthesize the material on women and credit has been, the task was daunting. Scholars have written so much directly on the subject in so many languages and so much more turns out to be pertinent in books and articles on related economic, social, religious, and intellectual developments in this vast period, that I have had not only to pick and choose but also to stop picking and choosing if the project was ever going to reach fruition. What I have synthesized, I think, gives a sound picture of certain central aspects of the history and sociology of women and credit. And I know of no other study of the subject on this scale. The intended audience of the book is research specialists interested in contextualizing their conclusions and educated general readers who want to get a sense of the limits of scholars' knowledge of the theme.

In order to achieve as broad a synthesis as possible I have combined the findings of various scholars in my own research specialty in medieval European history with the findings of students of ancient and early modern Europe and of various periods of Near Eastern, African, Asian, and American history. In some instances the studies encountered were bold yet tentative because the documentary base was thin; studies on Antiquity are a case in point. In other instances, the social scientific, feminist, and literary-critical methods employed by the researchers were initially unfamiliar to me and difficult of access as a social and legal historian of the Middle Ages. Moreover, at times, the issues addressed by students differed markedly from those addressed in traditional scholarship on my period. I tried to regard the challenge of synthesis presented by these differences positively, but I am aware that the selection of topics given fullest treatment in the book is colored by my training and temperament.

The study has emerged as a three-part "report" of sorts. Each part treats a fundamental issue of the activities of women in offering and obtaining credit. Part One takes up the rich theme of consumer loans, networks of female sociability, and the factors that encouraged, conditioned, and limited it—age, class, religion, ethnicity. Much of the data comes from the enormous amount of research done on medieval Europe, but I have made an effort to give this section a comparative dimension. Part Two, which chronologically continues the discussion in the preceding part, concerns women's roles in productive loans (investment and capital formation) in late medieval and early modern Europe, especially England, where credit transactions of this sort had a prominent place. Again, some effort has gone into comparing the English to continental European and other experiences. Part Three deals with women traders and credit. Although one goal of this part is to achieve a certain level of generality, the principal focus is on colonial and post-colonial women in sub-Saharan Africa, particularly West Africa, and the Caribbean: this choice for study reflects both the prominence of women in marketing in these regions and the extensive and high quality of scholarly work discussing their role. A brief conclusion suggests some of the persistent features and changing parameters in the history of credit—and women's roles in it—in industrial societies.

"Historical discussion of the economic role of women," Marjorie McIntosh reminds us, "has often been somewhat superficial." [12] Though addressing the scholarship on late medieval and early modern England, her remark applies equally well to other environments. It may seem to the reader that to undertake a relatively short synthetic study on the scale just sketched is to invite a similar criticism. What is it, after all, that women have in common among so many distinctive cultures that permits, let alone encourages, a synthesis of this sort? Equally important, what are the limitations to the study?

To answer these questions it may be valuable to explore a little more fully the theoretical underpinnings of a study of this sort. My basic argument is that synthesis, though dependent on generalization and, therefore, simplification, need not be intellectually superficial. By its very nature synthesis on the scale attempted here is *comparative* and can raise new questions on issues long considered closed and supply new insights into problems insularly treated. We must, of course, forswear assessing the quality of economic relationships in other societies and cultures in terms of their alleged deviation from our own as the perceived norm. [13] Indeed, if nothing else, synthesis on this scale can serve as a salutary reminder to us in the Western tradition that our own experience over time has been varied and cannot easily be "essentialized."

But there are other justifications for a synthesis of this sort. At the heart of them, as already remarked, is the recognition that the division of labor between the sexes is a common cultural phenomenon. The precise nature of the division, of course, differs from society to society and among the constitutive groups within each of these societies. The nature of economic exchange requires those who wish to produce goods or provide services to accumulate sufficient capital (or capital equipment) to initiate production or to obtain the education or support and protection necessary to provide services. This may seem a cold way of talking about women in unsophisticated economies acquiring the cash to buy the vats to brew their beer for an incipient market or the stove and wood to make meat pies to sell at a fair; it is a still colder way of talking about women who provide sexual services, accepting the necessity of enlisting pimps for their protection and that of their market. But cold or not, they are realities of everyday life in most historical and many contemporary societies.

Credit in the broadest sense of the term—belief in the willingness of the potential worker to work, the apprentice to learn, the entrepreneur to create the business she says she wants to create—is the key to opening up new possibilities for individual lives. In a patriarchal world, there is a differential distribution of credit in this broad sense: adult men, on average, have a great deal more than adult women. But credit is also a term that has a very restricted meaning, one that involves the willingness of a person of relative wealth to lend money to another person. In a place like Europe in the years 1000 to 1300, during which the traffic in money and commerce in general were considered morally problematic, it may not be surprising that women had a privileged role to play in certain forms of commercial transactions.[14] In a world where intimate social contact between the sexes is proscribed, as among the Muslim Hausa in West Africa, it will not be surprising that women maintain separate networks of providing credit among themselves.[15] And in cultures that privilege herding and fishing as male occupations, it will assuredly come as no surprise that women who do food preparation often do marketing as well and, therefore, take a leading role in credit transactions.[16]

These descriptions apply to various historical and contemporary societies and cultures (not just the ones mentioned) that thus put women into peculiar sets of relationships involving borrowing and lending. Neither the concept of "society" nor that of "culture" ought to be reified, of course. Individual actors have a great deal of play or flexibility available. The existence of such play does not mean that the story will necessarily be triumphalist, with women seeing the problems, cobbling together the best possible plan, and beating the "system." Such outcomes are at best occasionally achieved—and then only for limited groups of women—and we shall see why this is so in the pages that follow. One reason, however, should be mentioned now, namely, the fact that there have almost always been other groups (not necessarily exclusively male) that, because of their status, competed with women in general or with specific groups of women in the economy: Jews in medieval Europe; immigrant males in the marketplaces of colonial West Africa; Irish servants in the Caribbean islands of the nineteenth century.[17] All that I would argue at this point is that there are sufficient pressures on women's roles in the economy and in particular on their credit relationships in pre-industrial and developing societies to recommend a study of the scope offered in this book.

The limits of the undertaking in these pages should be obvious, one of them being evidence. It is not simply a question of the low rate of survival of evidence that once existed (which, as remarked, makes all studies of antiquity speculative). It is also the fact that the kinds of societies that we shall be most interested in studying were at best only partly literate; and insofar as scribes and notaries acted to preserve the actions of people in writing, they were biased toward recording the actions of men. Second, even where records are voluminous, there are problems. The developing societies that will concern us are a case in point. Because they were once colonial societies, the precious documentation from which their history must be written is tainted not merely by the bias toward men but by the skewed concerns of colonial recordkeeping in general—albeit in different ways, depending on whether the colonial impact was short or long, culminated in a large settler community or not, or effected the destruction of indigenous peoples and their replacement with slaves and indentured servants. Third, it is in the very nature of a "developing" society to produce records that will highlight the development process per se, that is, the kinds of cataclysmic changes associated with attempts at rapid industrialization and state building. Such documentation usually either ignores or dismisses longstanding ("traditional") economic arrangements, including those involving credit.[18]

There is a further danger related to this third consideration, namely, that readers of the developmental record will be seduced into romancing the past, simply because the problems inherent in the development process will appear to be so massive, tragic, and overwhelming. We will begin to imagine a past world that was almost idyllic in comparison, at least with regard to its human relationships. "Tradition" will not only be reified; it will be reified as a long lost friend, until every vestige of tradition is sanctified by scholarly prose.

To be sure, whether inherited credit arrangements were more humane and whether they can survive in periods when there are attempts at rapid economic development are important questions—questions that can and must be addressed without romance. But even if particular traditional (and humane) arrangements collapsed under rapid development, it would still be useful to see what arrangements took their place and how they were themselves informed and constrained by tradition. For women interacting among themselves and with men in the polyglot, poorly serviced post-colonial "megacities" of the Third World, access to credit remains a central concern.[19] Did traditions deeply constrain responses to these new forms of urban life? Among village families whose livelihood has been disrupted by the transformative effects of large scale permanent and cyclic male migration associated with rapid development, the question of who borrows or can borrow from whom is crucial for survival.[20] Did traditional village norms hold back creative responses to the new situation? Rapid economic development stimulates "shadow economies" and "black markets," which are sometimes—or so it has been alleged—more important than the so-called formal sector.[21] If such arrangements are even remotely as significant as has been argued, then we must wonder about their impact on matters of credit. What is the nature of "trust" in the black market? Do women behave in ways shaped primarily by custom or by the repressive hand of the state?[22]

Naturally, this book cannot be and will not attempt to be a comprehensive or systematic study of post-colonial megacities, massive labor migration, informal economies, state formation, dependency theory, or a myriad of other interesting phenomena like African and Caribbean markets, but these issues will be addressed—sometimes at length—when they are directly relevant to the problem of female access to and provision of credit. The book also cannot be an extended essay on patriarchy and hierarchy—their specific content in various cultures, their formative power, their limits—although almost every page implicitly or explicitly invokes some aspects of our understanding of the content, power, and limits of patriarchy and hierarchy as they impinge on lending and borrowing. Finally, this book cannot pretend to have captured in a study of credit anything like the essence of sexual conflict and cooperation in the pre-industrial and developing economies. Nevertheless, an understanding of the role of sex in such an important aspect of traditional life as credit relationships should contribute something to the ongoing re-examination of the issue in general. In any case, as noted earlier, to my knowledge no one has tried to tackle the question of women and credit in quite such a *longue durée* and for quite so many cultures. Without trying to go into detail about every cultural or social formation in which the credit relationships addressed here arose, I have struggled to make a reasonable effort to nuance my conclusions and to be frank about their limitations. Perhaps the study will stimulate others, better situated, to try to do more.

Notes

1. The major part of the writing of this study was completed while I was on leave from Princeton University and a Fellow of the Annenberg Research Institute for Judaic and Near Eastern Studies in Philadelphia, 1989–1990. I want to thank the former Director of the Institute, Professor Bernard Lewis, the other Fellows, and the learned and helpful staff, especially Dr. Vera Moreen, for making my tenure at the Institute a thoroughly delightful as well as stimulating experience. I would also like to thank my colleague, Robert Tignor. Small parts of the argument in the book have been presented before learned audiences at the conference on "Changing the Middle Ages: New Perspectives on Medieval Studies," Scripps College (March 1991), before the Fellows of the Shelby Cullom Davis Center for Historical Studies, Princeton University (April 1991), at the annual meeting of Rutgers and Princeton medievalists (October 1991), and at the conference, "The Middle Ages: One or Many," State University of New York, Albany (April 1992).

2. For example, for medieval Europe, see Herlihy 1990, 1–8, 25–39, 52–55. Cf. the division of labor in the "informal sector" of the African economy; Nelson 1979, 283–302.

3. Herlihy 1990, 1–12, 28–29, 34–39, 76–89.

4. Herlihy 1990, 91–97.

5. Vanja 1986, 147–59; Ennen 1985, 233–34.

6. Hafter 1985, 71–87.

7. Cf. Penn 1987, 1–15; Vanja 1986, 147–59.

8. Collins 1989, 461–63.

9. Cf. Herlihy 1990, 13–14, 112–14.

10. The phrase is from Tawney's "Introduction" to Thomas Wilson's *Discourse upon Usury*; Tawney 1925, 121.

11. Herlihy 1990, 154–80.

12. McIntosh 1986, 175.

13. See the cautionary remarks in Little 1975, 107–21.

14. See, for example, Jordan 1978, 53–55.

15. Coles 1991, 163–91.

16. See pp. 103–6.

17. See pp. 19, 98, 111–12.

18. Lewis 1982, 108–9.

19. For the usage, "megacities," see Buvinić and Yudelman 1989, 11. See also Youssef and Hetler 1983, 237.

20. Gordon 1980–1981, 59–76, considers the effect of cyclic migration on women in the recent history of Lesotho. See also, more generally, Youssef and Hetler 1983, 237.

21. On the basis of work on Zaire, MacGaffey 1988, 161, argues that "urban women are as invisible in official reports and statistics as rural women. Many of the most successful and lucrative economic activities of women in towns and cities go unrecognized because they are carried out in the second economy, that sector of the total economy which evades the control of the state."

22. Hansen 1989, 143–60, downplays the importance of the state as a shaper of female participation in the black market; her conclusion is based on a study of female traders in Lusaka, Zambia. For a wide-ranging theoretical discussion of the role of the state with regard to women and development (including problems of credit), see Everett 1989, 152–76; her focus is India.

Part One

Consumption Loans and Networks of Sociability in the Middle Ages

A lmost all the men and women who have studied so-called "primitive" societies (those organized along kinship lines and not widely employing money as a medium of exchange) agree that life in these societies requires at least some use of credit. To be sure, the credit employed is of the most rudimentary type (so rudimentary that a few scholars doubt its right to the name).[1] And one loses little in terms of analytic precision in discussing primitive credit in the language of gift exchange: the creditor is in effect a gift giver who merely expects a "delayed" reciprocal gift from the recipient.[2] The value (symbolic or otherwise) of the gift finally reciprocated may be remarkably inferior to that of the original, yet it may still be acceptable and appropriate if the initial giver chooses to regard it as a sufficient acknowledgment of his or her superior status. Indeed, whenever such an acknowledgment takes place, it is probably less proper to talk of credit or of gifts, pristinely conceived as free will offerings without strings attached (presuming such gifts can ever exist), than of the creation of clientage. Or perhaps, it is more proper to speak of all three as manifestations of the same need to establish and maintain social networks. Whatever the case, we shall see that the relationship between gift, credit, and patronage/clientage remains close in all periods for which documentation exists.

Unfortunately, few early periods, not even ancient Greece and Rome, offer rich caches of information on credit, and what they do provide requires very cautious interpretation.[3] An older view, associated with Michael Rostovtzeff, saw in ancient Greece a thoroughly credit using society, with regard to both consumption loans and productive loans. Among free farmers moneylending was allegedly ubiquitous.[4] For a while Rostovtzeff's case seemed compelling not so much because of the Greek evidence he brought to bear (precious little) but from the fact that his argument about Greece contained bits and pieces of evidence from other ancient societies. Thus his readers learned that private banking and moneylending were widespread in Ptolemaic Egypt. He also characterized Hellenistic societies like the Seleucid East of the fourth century B.C. as ones in which entrepreneurs might accumulate considerable wealth from moneylending. And he pointed to the temples of first- and second-century B.C. Caria (in southwestern Asia Minor) as institutional moneylenders. Credit, in other words, seemed pervasive.[5]

Rome, to Rostovtzeff, was also—and increasingly as its power grew— a credit-using society.[6] Indeed, in his own phrase credit came to be "fully developed" in the Empire as a whole; and in parts of it, such as Asia Minor, moneylending became a routine if "subsidiary source of income" for the typical prosperous farmer.[7]

More recent historians of Greece and Rome have taken a much less sanguine view, even of Rostovtzeff's assertions on productive lending.[8] Although with regard to consumption lending everyone acknowledges that there must have been innumerable, perhaps gift-like, transactions, it now appears that the evidence is insufficient to sustain the sweeping generalizations suggested by Rostovtzeff about the prominent (or common) role of moneylending as an income-producing activity among people of relatively low social status. Indeed, nothing seems certain anymore.[9]

The Middle Ages: Background

Historiographical developments regarding the place of credit in the Middle Ages have had a decidedly different trajectory. Whatever the level of sophistication of the ancient economy in its various manifestations over the centuries, earlier generations of medievalists insisted that the centuries immediately after the fall of Imperial administration in the West experienced a significant regression and, a fortiori, a restriction in the forms and use of credit. Scholars attributed a "natural economy" to the early Middle Ages in the West (the "Dark Ages"), an economy in which barter played perhaps the key role in exchange, and exchange itself was minimal. By the early twentieth century, however, economic historians were successfully challenging this picture: the political and administrative decline of Imperial authority in the West, they contended, witnessed no parallel collapse of the economy.[10] This challenge was relevant, in discussions of credit, primarily to earlier statements about productive lending. These historians regarded consumption lending as unworthy of study or, if not unworthy, at least unimportant to the debate. What mattered, after all, was the question of economic development; consumer credit, they asserted strongly, could have had little to do with the secular growth of the medieval economy anyway.[11]

Nonetheless, elite *arguments* about consumer credit were relevant to questions of economic growth, since these arguments, which contested the morality of charging interest, impinged on any assessment of the willingness of medieval merchants and banks to invest. At its most developed—in its scholastic form—the moral analysis of usury was a complex attempt to strike a balance between long-standing practices and biblical injunctions against lending at interest.[12] Authorities did not all speak with one voice, of course. Some rejected the morality of charging any interest whatsoever: they found support in an argument about the nature of time. Money was not a crop or piece of machinery. Its intrinsic value was minimal. Interest, therefore, from their point of view, was a charge for the use (*usura*/usury, in its non-pejorative sense) of money over time.[13] Indeed, interest purchased time. On the other hand, no one could purchase time, which, like knowledge, was a gift of God.[14]

Arguments like these were the most radical, and if applied would have led to the prohibition of most loans. Many authorities, however, took a different approach. They conceded that productive loans—investments—were a necessary evil, maybe even a good. What they rarely conceded was that consumption loans, which they associated with the mulcting of poor people at a time of distress, were legitimate. Yet, legitimate or not, they seemed ineradicable. Therefore a different kind of concession glossed the practice. Lending at interest to distressed persons for the profit of the lender was reprehensible; but the alternative, for the borrower in distress, might be starvation or death. Such lending might thus be licit, but Christians, the people of God, should not practice it. Christian rulers and their, often clerical, advisers, however, almost everywhere permitted Jews to practice it.

Although pariah-group lending occurs in many cultures,[15] the specific argument in medieval Europe for permitting Jews to make such loans turned on biblical passages that implied that it was unacceptable for brothers to take interest from brothers, but acceptable to do so from strangers (Deut. 23.19–20). Universalizing notions of Christianity as well as a specific New Testament text forbidding interest (Luke 6.35) problematized the brother/stranger exception in Christian thought and always created tension. But, with some misgivings, apologists recognized that there was little alternative to such lending if poor Christians were to have access to needed cash and products at difficult times in their lives. In most other societies where there has been an ethical or religious antipathy toward the charging of interest, the same concession has been grudgingly made or, at least, the market in consumption loans was winked at unless it became exploitative.[16] In medieval Europe, the other side of the coin to this concession was the continued strong denunciation of Christian moneylending. Indeed, whenever Christian apologists were confronted with evidence of Christians lending to Christians at interest, they routinely stigmatized it as a form of "judaizing."[17]

Over time, recurrent misgivings about the legitimacy of Jews lending to Christians at interest stimulated a whole set of reproaches. Polemicists lamented the plight of "miserable persons," that is, those entitled to pity, whom circumstances forced to go into debt to Jews: the *miserabiles* were classically defined as widows, orphans, and the sick.[18] Polemicists also chafed with the knowledge that Crusaders, whose mission to recover and sustain the Holy Land was sacred, went into heavy debt to the Jews to finance their voyages to the East. They particularly condemned what we would now call compound interest, which took the form of penalty payments for failing to pay interest on schedule. "Usury of usuries" or "usury upon usury" they called it, from around the beginning of the thirteenth century.[19] Secular princes picked up the terminology in the fourteenth century as they too increasingly turned against the Jews.[20]

The ideological pressure against moneylending and the psychological pressure deliberately put on Christian moneylenders and any Jews who cared to listen were intense. Dream interpretation manuals that local cunning men and women may have used in practicing their craft show a marked willingness to construe the objects seen in their customers' nightmares as the expression of secret fears either of exploiting the poor through abusive credit or of becoming dependent on moneylenders.[21] Why should this not have been the case, when artists rendered the usurer—miserly and avaricious—as a beast and represented his "profession" with scatological images?[22] A few poems that have some structural features in common with lyrical poetry survive that represent usurers as "schizoid" personalities, frightened sinners, devoted to prayer yet so given over to avarice as to be unable to pray without their thoughts recurring to the unseemly and unnatural pleasures of usury. The sentence, "Forgive us our debts as we forgive our debtors," in the version of the Lord's Prayer prayed by the usurer in one such poem induces a grievous crisis.[23]

Various euphemisms were employed to mask the dirty work of "usury," various loopholes in the prescriptions against it were exploited, and many creative collusive practices managed to circumvent lingering prohibitions. This was true in medieval Christendom and, as we might expect, in many other "traditional" societies.[24] This may suggest some of the psychological tension that frequently accompanied the most abusive forms of distress loans. Workaday manuals composed in order to help parish priests deal with the routine problems they faced devote an inordinate amount of space to what amounts to counseling moneylenders through prayer.[25] Exempla, the moralistic stories stuck into medieval sermons to remind the listeners that the wages of sin is death, often depicted the conversion of usurers or their terrible end in the absence of repentance.[26] At the very end of the Middle Ages (or during the Renaissance, if one prefers), we find Rabelais, through the character Epistemon, imagining usurers being punished in hell,

> all busy looking for rusty pins and old nails in the gutters of the streets, as you see rascals doing in this world. But a hundredweight of such old iron is worth no more than a scrap of bread there; and yet there's a very poor supply of it. So the poor misers sometimes go for more than three weeks without eating a crumb or a morsel, and working day and night . . . [27]

How did women fit into the world of consumer credit in the Middle Ages? Did their roles differ from rural to urban areas? Under what circumstances could and did women borrow money? Did they suffer the same opprobrium when they lent money as men did? How did men and women apportion the market between themselves? Were female moneylenders "professionals?" Did female creditors and borrowers have distinctive financial and social networks within which they operated? However distinct the networks, did they transcend ethnic and religious boundaries? These and related questions are the principal concern of the first part of this study.

Women and Consumer Credit: The Data

Because unpaid debts were the object of incessant litigation and because illegal (usurious) lending activities were frequently the target of special investigations in the Middle Ages, a considerable body of documentation has survived on these questions, at least from the thirteenth century onward.[28] It is good to be wary of taking these records of bad debts and illegal activities at face value, that is, as indications of the routine functioning of the credit market, but most historians have been careful on this matter.

The types of lending and borrowing revealed in these records vary. Most rural court rolls, particularly from manors or villages, are full of cases that allude to purchases on credit or to indebtedness caused by employers failing to pay wages (the employer, that is, holding back the wage earner's pay as a no-interest loan). It is doubtful that the predominance of matters of this kind in litigation reflects the fact that credit in general was similarly weighted toward these two sorts of transactions, even though some historians insist that "most peasant credit probably did not involve cash advances" in the thirteenth century.[29] The difficulty in accepting this conclusion lies in the fact that cash advances would typically imply lending at interest. Some unrepaid, interest-bearing cash advances would simply be too small to be worth litigating about and, therefore, would not appear in these sources.[30] In other instances, it is hard to imagine a moneylender seeking recovery in court of the principal of a loan on which a borrower had defaulted after *long*, if still incomplete, payment of legal interest. Indeed, it might be wise on the moneylender's part to try to avoid public disclosure of bad debts on those rare occasions when the interest paid in the aggregate exceeded the size of the principal. Finally, moneylenders who wanted to collect on loans on which they had charged illegal interest could not bring actions to court; yet it goes without saying that there were creditors who offered loans at illegal rates to people who, for whatever reason, were unable to get credit elsewhere.

The great bulk of the evidence that has survived, therefore, would—unmediated and unsupplemented—undoubtedly provide us with a very skewed picture, not just with regard to the kinds of transactions but also with regard to the gender profile of the lenders and borrowers.[31] For it is well known that the court rolls in general, even if they preserve some of the stories of women's lending and borrowing,[32] are biased toward the activities of men. This does not mean that the data are insufficient to tell the tale that needs to be told. In the first place, other valuable sets of documents exist, sometimes no less weighty in their bulk than the great rolls of village courts.

There were, for example, special princely sponsored investigations into illegal lending, particularly that practiced by Jews in rural and urban areas, and those that have left evidence behind have been elaborately studied.[33] Municipal courts throughout Europe have yielded considerable treasures.[34] Royal courts offer a little more.[35] Notarial records are remarkably helpful for both the urban and rural society of the south of Europe.[36] And there are also wonderful serendipities in the collections of original bonds and account books that have survived for Bavaria, the Rhineland, England, and France.[37]

The people who provided the small loans that were needed by poor people or people temporarily short of cash to pay the expenses for a christening party or wedding feast, for buying food until a breadwinner was paid, managed to find work, or got well, or for burying a relative were a varied lot.[38] Typical of pre-modern societies, not all of them were "professionals," by any means.[39] Sometimes itinerants, men—Christian or Jewish—who peddled their wares from village to village, offered credit to trusted customers, a practice, again, common to many pre-modern cultures outside Europe.[40] Clerics, too, either unimpressed by the ideology to which they paid lip service or concerned but overcome by greed, put out a little money at interest.[41] There *may* have been a charitable dimension to their activity; often it is hard to tell.[42]

Monastic houses and their inmates (monks and lay brothers) were on occasion in the business of moneylending.[43] So were, more regularly, inn- and tavern keepers, craftsmen, notaries, and immigrants who were denied other means of economic livelihood.[44] People suspected of heresy were also ostracized in many communities, forced from respectable pursuits, and reduced to moneylending, or took it up precisely because they held the "orthodox" in contempt, strangers to the Truth, the minions of Satan.[45] Where two or more pariah groups existed, like immigrants and Jews, they sometimes divided the market among themselves—not deliberately but according to the relative disdain in which each was held by the dominant group—the uttermost of the out-groups servicing the least creditworthy among the borrowers.[46] Sometimes the most wealthy gentlemen extended loans to those in need whom they regarded as their dependents. Thomas Sutton, one of the great Tudor-Stuart moneylenders, a man at home in the heady world of high finance, "in the area that he considered his home . . . lent money to husbandmen, country clergymen, and shopkeepers." Locals thought well of him for his generous condescension and consulted him on the difficulties they faced in dealing with the wider world.[47]

Women moneylenders who made small consumption loans were almost as varied. There is little evidence of them as itinerant moneylenders, but aside from this the record is full. Upper class Christian women appear to act in much the same way as Thomas Sutton during the same period.[48] For medieval England, scholars have recovered documentary evidence of female village lenders, Christians, of significantly less lofty status as well.[49] They included pawnbrokers and alewives who did pawnbroking on the side in rural Salisbury and metropolitan London.[50] The same may be said of medieval France (including Paris), Germany, Denmark, Italy, Russia, and so on.[51] Governmental decrees and apologetic literature refer repeatedly to Christian women who made small loans at interest or who were known as usurers.[52] Even nuns, as we shall see, engaged in this kind of moneylending, though with unique refinements and intentions.[53]

Occasionally, the data bases permit us to get some sense of the proportional representation of Christian women as moneylenders. The village court rolls of Writtle, an English village make the proportion 14 percent of all lenders.[54] Across the Channel in Flanders a similar proportion seems to hold: fourteenth-century Ghent accounted 16 percent of its moneylenders as women.[55] In contemporary Montpellier far to the south, the proportion, so far as we can tell, was 11.3 percent.[56]

Women and Consumer Credit: Status

The existence of Christian women as moneylenders in the proportions indicated (though these may not be generalizable throughout rural and urban Europe in the Middle Ages) immediately raises an important question. Were these women professionals whose fundamental business (and perhaps livelihood) was moneylending? The preponderance of the evidence would suggest that, exceptions aside, they were not. Rather, Christian women lent money on the side. A very old pattern was repeated here in which women involved in trade, given their access to ready cash, extended credit on purchases, gave cash advances to good customers, or accepted articles at pawn.[57] This pattern persisted throughout the Middle Ages. Tradeswomen, after all, could legally engage in almost all kinds of business permitted to men. There were alewives and female innkeepers who could lend money, and many widows supplemented their earnings from their late husbands' businesses or homesteads by putting out cash at interest.[58]

The Jewish woman who made what we would call consumption loans in the Middle Ages has been more thoroughly studied, including her access to and control of resources.[59] Although some of these women, like the majority of their Christian counterparts, only lent money informally or as a sideline or continued their husbands' businesses briefly on widowhood, most of them were professionals.[60] The explanation for the difference is simple. By the time our evidence becomes abundant in the thirteenth century, Jews—men and women—were largely restricted to the business of moneylending or pawnbroking. This was not true everywhere at the end of the thirteenth century in Europe (particularly not in southern Europe),[61] but it was very common and would become ever more common in those areas where Jews continued to reside in the later Middle Ages. Being the predominant way to earn an income, moneylending was an enterprise that was carefully cultivated.

Jewish women were very active moneylenders in nearly every region where Jews lived. In medieval England, before the expulsion of 1290, the evidence testifies to the widespread presence of the Jewish woman moneylender.[62] Across the Channel the situation was similar. About one-third of the total number of Jews known to have been lending money in northern France in the thirteenth century were women.[63] Somewhere between 30 percent and 50 percent represents the proportion also in northern France in the fourteenth century.[64] A very similar impression has been reached for the south, as, for example, in the late medieval Principality of Orange on the Rhône.[65] In German-speaking regions of Europe, the Jewish woman moneylender was ubiquitous.[66]

On the southern side of the Pyrenees extensive research documents the same phenomenon. Sometimes the data, being fragmentary, do not permit the confident assertion of precise proportions of female to male lenders, but the frequency with which we encounter the Jewish female lender is striking. In fourteenth-century Navarre Jewish widows played a very energetic role as creditors.[67] And while widows seem always and everywhere in the medieval period to form an important component of women engaged in business or having prominent parts in public forums,[68] the evidence on Jews suggests that married women were almost as likely to be engaged in moneylending as their widowed counterparts. Sometimes they even had separate businesses or at least serviced different markets from those of their husbands who were also professional moneylenders. Thirteenth-century Catalonia, to give merely one example, provides us with evidence of the "extensive economic activities [including moneylending] in which some Jewish women engaged independently of their husbands."[69]

The massive effort to recover all the documentation on the major and many minor Jewish settlements in Italy, led by Simonsohn, furnishes us with still more revealing data.[70] Again it is not always possible to be confident about percentages, but the remarkable activity of Italian Jewish women in economic life as moneylenders is undeniable.[71] Fragmentary evidence of loan transactions from late medieval Ancona shows approximately 15 percent women creditors among all Jewish creditors.[72] Piedmontese and Savoyard government records routinely refer to Jewish creditors of both sexes in decrees—*judeis utriusque sexus*.[73] In sixteenth-century Cremona, it was expected that a moneylender would be *ebreo od ebrea*.[74] Even where Christian authorities had given monopolies to individual (male) Jews in particular Italian towns to lend money, women might (illegally) intrude themselves[75] and in fact become worrisome competitors as the petition of a Jewish Pavian monopolist, dated 17 June 1477, indicates.[76] Finally, the fifteenth-century community of Valona on the Albanian coast, a community of Iberian and Italian immigrant Jews from the persecutions in the West, replicated the pattern: women in this community lent money at interest just as they and their ancestors had done for centuries in their homelands.[77]

Whatever Jewish women accomplished in servicing these villages and towns (a theme to which we shall return), the differences between them and Jewish men in carrying out the same tasks should not be exaggerated. One advantage, for example, that Jewish men had over most Christians, male or female, and almost certainly over Jewish women in general in the Middle Ages was literacy. At first glance we might expect that this difference had a profound effect on their respective lending practices. Yet it is not unthinkable that most Christian *professional* lenders and Jewish women of the same occupation enjoyed functional literacy and numeracy. Even if Jewish female creditors were not literate, it is not clear that they would have been disadvantaged by the fact or would have behaved in radically different ways because of it. After all, since Jewish men could be employed as scribes and many businesses were family-run, it was not absolutely necessary for women to acquire these skills.[78] It is rare indeed that the records reveal a Jewish woman unable to handle the routine writing of bonds or forced to seek help outside her family circle to do so.[79]

Yet, though we should not exaggerate differences, we must not downplay them either. Neither Christian women nor Jewish women, as a group, seem to have benefited in terms of status from their roles as moneylenders, unlike, say, some Italian moneylenders. (To be sure, the prestige of the latter was itself frequently tenuous.) From time to time men and other women must have regarded female moneylenders' accomplishments and their wealth (when they controlled it themselves) with envy, but there is no evidence whatever that the level of activity and capabilities of women as moneylenders had a subversive effect on the overall hierarchies of medieval society.[80] One possible reason for the nonthreatening character of this particular form of female "empowerment" has something to do with the market these women served. It was not merely the small loan market, but a particular and not very prized slice of it, namely, the very smallest loans—what might be called, to anticipate a bit, the "domestic" part of the market.

Of course, women occasionally made large loans. (We shall have to return to this issue in the discussion of investment in Part Two.) But their specialty was small loans and, indeed, the smallest of the small, usually only one-half to one-third the size of loans made by male moneylenders. Evidence from northern France, England, Italy, and Catalonia on Jewish moneylenders appears to support this conclusion.[81] And a wide array of evidence on Christian moneylenders appears to do so as well.[82]

The distinction to be drawn is this. Men who lent money frequently served people who were caught at particularly difficult times in the agricultural cycle. They also served people who needed to replace or repair machinery that could not be replaced or repaired with ordinary household help—plows, harnesses, harrows, lathes, and so on. Breakdowns in equipment often corresponded to the cycles of the work year: it was preferable to have plows repaired off-season, sometime in the winter, when extra money became available from marketing or service. But one could put off having the repairs made for just so long (that is, until right before planting began). Moreover, new repairs were needed soon afterward as a result of wear and tear during peak periods of summer and fall plowing. An enormous amount of information has been amassed that shows the cyclic character of lending and borrowing that this sort of scenario implies.[83] The pattern does not markedly differ whether the lenders are urban or rural, because urban lenders serviced rural hinterlands and the rhythms of rural life profoundly conditioned the cycles of the medieval and early modern European urban economy.[84]

For most peasant and artisanal producers the loans needed to purchase seed corn, restock cattle, and repair equipment were small and were repaid, whether to Jews or Christians, over a short term, usually no more than a very few months. Although these loans may have been overlaid with elaborate guarantees for repayment,[85] they are not usually distinguished in our sources from more informal consumption loans per se, which were also short term.[86] But small as they were they were almost certainly larger than the domestic loans that we normally associate with consumer credit. Categorized as business loans, they imparted to the men who made them something of the emerging (though limited) prestige of businessmen. Although men serviced the domestic market, catering to people who were unemployed or merely short of cash,[87] they did not do so exclusively or as exclusively as women seem to have done.

Networks of Sociability

Many of the borrowers involved in these domestic loans were women. Small scale moneylending was almost always informal in medieval Europe, whether the lenders and borrowers were male or female.[88] (The major exception to this statement involves the pawn banks of late medieval Italy, to which we shall soon address ourselves.)[89] This informality undermined all legalistic attempts to prevent adult women, married or otherwise under the juridical "cover" of a male, from making contractual obligations without their husbands' or other appropriate men's consent.[90] Tradeswomen, widows, and spinsters, of course, were not even prohibited by law from making contracts. A fourteenth-century Italian manuscript illumination pictorially sums up the situation by depicting a large number of women (including a nun) and their children calling on the moneylenders of a town.[91]

It was natural that women as the managers of their households (as wives, widows, eldest daughters, spinsters) would disproportionately be the people to seek out domestic loans, those for necessities or family festivals. And scholars have had no trouble finding them doing just this. To be sure, most of the evidence concerns Christian women borrowers, and it is on them that we shall have to focus our discussion. But more needs to be known about the Jews—men or women—as borrowers for consumption or in distress. Even though there were community mechanisms among the Jews to succor the poor,[92] that such borrowing occurred is not in doubt: whether it was rare or frequent is.[93]

Whether it was exploitative or charitable is also in dispute. Rabbis in late medieval Italy denounced the practice, suggesting that it often had disagreeable overtones.[94] And Béatrice Leroy believes that she has found examples in Navarre of exploitative practices.[95] But Aaron Kirschenbaum has argued persuasively that many such loans ought to be regarded as a species of charity.[96] Even well-intentioned "charitable" lending, however, if this is what it was, could go amiss and end up in court or worse.[97] What is at stake in the debate is the truth or falsity of the profoundly held belief among students of Jewish history that the solidarity of the Jewish community (or communities) was too privileged an ideal and too crucial for survival, in the hostile environment of medieval Christendom, to permit members of the community to jeopardize it by exploiting their coreligionists who were in distress. The evidence increasingly points to the fact that insofar as the Jewries survived, they did so despite rather than in the absence of the social and personal rifts associated with distress loans and other forms of "exploitation": "La cohésion communautaire n'interdit pas un clivage social."[98]

As indicated, it is very difficult at this stage in the scholarship to pursue these issues or to stake out the precise role of women in Jewish society as borrowers for domestic consumption, let alone to explore the social dynamics of their role. For Christian women, however, this is possible, at least to some degree. And what is discoverable may have implications for women of both groups who were obliged to borrow in order to survive or make ends meet. The data cover the whole range of social categories, from rustics to noble women, and a host of regions, from Scotland to Germany to the Castilian frontier with Islam.[99] It should come as no surprise, given the domestic nature of most loans to women, that the average amount of money borrowed by a woman in medieval Europe in any transaction was likely to be significantly less than that borrowed by a man, perhaps only half or a third as much, in any body of data covering all types of small loans.[100] Nor should it be surprising that an enormous number of transactions involve woman-to-woman exchange.[101]

As was the case with men, the money that these women borrowed was often secured by credit in the widest sense, trustworthiness.[102] The rural and small town environments in which most Europeans lived cultivated strong neighborly goodwill and equally strong neighborly hatreds. Where goodwill obtained, some lenders, even professionals and, again, male or female, Jewish or Christian, demanded nothing but the promise of a friend as "collateral" from trustworthy borrowers who had repaid their debts properly in the past.[103] At times some of these transactions between friends and kin probably were not even monetized: "Don't thank me. Just do something for me when I need it."[104] The distinction between loans and charity can again become hard to make.

The mere charging of interest probably did undermine the purely charitable aspect of these loans. A borrower might be happy to receive money but she was not necessarily happy to pay back more than she borrowed. All the same, this consideration can be given too much weight. Too often scholars have annualized interest rates on these small loans.[105]

As an annual rate of return, two pennies per pound per week (a common formula) was high: 43.33 percent. But in northern France where, say, a forester made six pounds a year in the thirteenth century, it is highly dubious that he or his wife would borrow what amounts to two months' wages.[106] Domestic loans were small. They were frequently accounted in shillings and even pence. And they were short term. They were repaid in two or three weeks or two or three months.[107] They might be stretched out a little longer (necessity was a hard taskmaster at times). So we find innumerable references in the sources, whether regarding men or women, to *prolongationes*, *prorogationes*, *elongamenta*, *elongationes*, and *provisiones* of loans.[108] This could cause problems, generate animosity: delays for the length of time desired could not always have been granted; and the very requests might have been resented by the lenders.[109] Nonetheless, almost all small loans were repaid in far less than a year.[110] In absolute terms, then, the amount of interest paid could be quite reasonable.[111] It might still irk the borrower to pay it, but interest was not necessarily the fearful burden that some scholars have made it.

In any case, there is no doubt whatever that strong networks, supported by kinship, friendship and respect, often existed within the world of male lending and borrowing, among women borrowers and lenders, and sometimes among women and men involved together in credit transactions. Like all discussions of networks of sociability, the problem is not in establishing their existence. Overlapping patterns of borrowing and lending are easily documentable: the rustic temporarily strapped for cash one harvestide could be a benefactor to a former benefactor the next.[112] There is not even any difficulty in imputing some sort of psychological or social force to these networks. Already in the late Middle Ages one could wax rhapsodic about their power to bind communities together, at least when the relationships implied in the networks were reciprocal and egalitarian, that is, when lenders one day could call on their former clients the next, if need be, without shame or embarrassment. As Panurge, the alternately swaggering and sniveling companion of Rabelais's Pantagruel, puts it:

> [I]magine to yourself another world in which everyone lends and everyone owes, where all are debtors and all are lenders. Oh, what a harmony there will be in the regular motions of the heavens. . . . Among mankind peace, love, affection, fidelity, repose, banquets, joy, gladness, gold, silver, small change, chains, rings, and merchandise will pass from hand to hand. No lawsuits, no war, no strife; no one there will be a usurer, nor a glutton, nor a miser, nor a refuser. . . . All men will be good, all will be just. Oh,

happy world! Oh, happy people in that world, three times and four times blest.[113]

The real problem is that networks were never like this: they were always unbalanced, skewed in their reciprocity, biased toward one group or another. This unhappy reality is probably why Rabelais puts the peroration quoted above in the mouth of such a duplicitous, ironic, and ultimately baffling character as Panurge. The task for us is to show why and how the relations of lender and borrower and the networks created by these relations differed (or were skewed) according as the people involved differed in class, ethnicity, confession, and gender. This is, indeed, "a complicated question,"[114] but one that deserves an attempt at an answer. Here the attempt—partial and tentative, to be sure—will be made by means of a close analysis of a few examples. The analysis will show, it is hoped, that networks involving women frequently responded in distinctly different ways to social and economic pressures, distinctly different from those involving only men did or can reasonably be presumed to have done. It will also try to show in what circumstances and under what pressures these networks fractured, that is, to what extent female involvement in credit transactions undermined various solidarities within medieval communities.

There was undoubtedly a domestic "world" in which women interacted almost exclusively with other women. There were economic and social environments within this world in which credit, however, played almost no role. R. H. Britnell in a study of late medieval Colchester in England, for example, has noticed that women had something of a special role on the temporal and spatial periphery of the Colchester market as forestallers, that is, as illegal brokers of produce before the marketplace opened.[115] His picture, which reveals forestallers purchasing from producers at lower prices than might have been obtained by the producers themselves in the marketplace, seems generalizable.[116]

This practice made sense on two levels. It liberated petty producers (who had intended to sell the goods themselves) to return to work at home, and it sometimes delivered into those producers' hands more money than they could receive from a licensed vendor—had they intended to deal with one—who was in a position to strike sharper deals. The practice could also benefit local consumers, because forestallers, by not charging for the market tolls, booth charges, and sales taxes that licensed vendors had to add to their bills, sold at prices inferior to those of the latter. P. J. P. Goldberg is positively rhapsodic about the female huckster who was "able to supply poorer townsfolk unable to purchase by bulk in the formal market place . . . [S]he performed a necessary function supplying the needs of that silent majority [!] of medieval urban society."[117] The problem was that there was no quality control of forestallers' products and not much redress for the customer if the merchandise turned out to be shoddy, spoiled, or on the turn. Moreover, the loss of business in the formal marketplace could cause honest stallholders to raise prices.[118]

On the one hand, many forestallers were wives of "marginal" stallholders (licensed vendors), those who for one reason or another were at a disadvantage with regard to competition with other vendors. These women, who frequently sold to other very poor women who could not afford the prices (and, therefore, benefit from the regularities) of the market-place were pitiable people, hanging "around lane ends in the hope of turning a quick penny." They had, in Britnell's words, "disreputable ways of going on," in the black and shadow market (in the economic sense) in which they functioned. He concludes that most of the forestallers were about as poor as their customers: "their misdemeanors were more a strategy for survival than a monopolistic conspiracy."[119]

On the other hand, Hutton found that in Shrewsbury many forestallers were unattached women or wives of fishermen, in many cases outsiders to the community.[120] Whether as wives of marginal stallholders (Britnell's model) or "aliens" of a sort (Hutton's), it is inconceivable that credit (*either* cash advances from forestallers to producers *or* delayed payment for forestallers on purchases from producers or for customers on purchases from forestallers) was a major aspect of this largely female network. The giving and obtaining of credit, in other words, starts with the presumption of goodwill and trust. The marginal world of forestalling in the villages and small towns of medieval Europe could not have been entirely without these, but it would be ludicrous and counterintuitive to believe that forestalling cultivated these virtues. If we are to explore credit in female networks we will have to look elsewhere than the black and shadow markets served by forestallers.

We have seen from court roll evidence, notarial records and the like that with regard to domestic loans women seem very often to have borrowed from women. This pattern is recognizable in other pre-modern cultures as well.[121] Wives often attested in the evidence that has come down to us that it was they who carried out the routine tasks of making payments to moneylenders. They were repeatedly in contact with the female moneylenders, as they paid the weekly interest that was required. Like the illumination described earlier that shows women and children visiting the moneylenders, documentary evidence also attests to women taking their young children with them on their periodic visits to the people from whom they borrowed. This occurred even when the loan had been made across confessional lines, as, for example, when the moneylender was a Jew and the borrower a Christian.[122]

Within this world impressions were formed by children that would inform their lifelong attitudes toward moneylenders and Jews. We may think of the process positively, with the children learning to apprise themselves of different cultures within their society and learning to appreciate how people from within those separate cultures might reach out to help their mothers, for the extending of loans could certainly be considered helpful. Far more important, I think, are the circumstances surrounding these loans. Many were distress loans. Children, therefore, observed their mothers negotiating with moneylenders at those most vulnerable times. Omniscient, powerful Christian parents (omniscient and powerful in the eyes of their young children) would almost necessarily have appeared weak.

This appearance of weakness was doubly harmful when the moneylender was Jewish. It meant that Jews and Judaism in general and the Jewry to which Christians repaired to pay their debts were associated with the humiliation of Christian parents. The word "humiliation" is not too strong: inevitably the Christian children were often witnesses to quarrels, such as that which followed a mother's inability to secure or obtain as large a loan as she wanted or a moneylender's refusal to offer as much as the mother had hoped for on an article to be pawned.[123] At times, perhaps because of earlier defaults, lenders must simply have said to some needy women that they could not help them out. We can hardly, if ever, know, but we can plausibly imagine the sort of conversation that a parent had with a child after this kind of failure or partial failure. The language of that conversation—remembered, repeated, confirmed by the stories of other people—inevitably colored the mental universe of those who heard it, and it would help shape or inform all later "discourse." The social world of female lending and borrowing, on one level evidence of benign reciprocity, was riven with potential for destructive impulses.

At its most benign, the world of female lending and borrowing was, however, capable of overcoming some prejudices in a way that was improbable in the social networks inhabited by men. Women could call, for example, on the reservoir of their respectability from performing honestly in credit transactions with other women, even across confessional lines, to help surmount prejudices that were disabling their husbands' business ventures.[124] (The process is unlikely to have been reversible.) But the most suggestive evidence for this is contained in the research published by Marjorie McIntosh in 1988 on the medieval manor of Havering, on the outskirts of London; and this evidence allows us to test the relative power of gender and ethnicity. There, in Havering, many immigrants from Flanders took up residence in the late Middle Ages in order to enter the cloth industry and trade. They were alienated from their hosts, as the immigrants of many communities were.[125] Yet the women of these immigrant communities frequently borrowed from English women. The immigration overall was a response to the growing commercialization or even "proto-industrialization" of the London economy. The expanding economy produced larger and larger enterprises, and, then, in their wake or lockstep with them, more professional moneylending with a market and concern for much larger loans.

This market on the supply side was dominated by Englishmen and their interests, and it was resented to some extent by Flemings against whom the English discriminated. Moreover, the rapidly developing economy that supported this explosion in the credit market was volatile. It suffered sharp setbacks and great surges, which imparted to the histories of many immigrant families an appalling precariousness. So even as new, more masculine credit networks accentuating class and ethnic differences became prominent, the older pattern of small domestic consumption loans, and especially of women-to-women loans, across ethnic lines persisted in sustaining vulnerable immigrant households. What was the nature of face-to-face relations of lending and borrowing in this environment? How did Flemish husbands value their wives' ability to hold together households by appealing to English women when temporary crashes occurred in an otherwise robust economy? One thing seems certain; however difficult relations between the two ethnic groups were, there was a level at which, among the women, the ethnic barrier could be breached. This is not a description of a love feast, but it does suggest the existence of a distinct outlook among the women toward economic difficulties.[126]

Another example of a kind of special configuration of female involvement in credit which has a decidedly benign aura about it concerns nuns. Here we see how a particular group of women, caught up in a strong religious network, used credit to enrich the ties of genial dependency within that network. Here, in all sorts of ways, we see goodwill underpinning lending and lending emerging as an act of charity. Nunneries, with a few exceptions, were notoriously underendowed in the Middle Ages. Consequently, their role in extending credit was circumscribed. Nonetheless, some nuns and nunneries did have a peculiar role in small loan transactions. The evidence has been explored most thoroughly for Italy. We can leave aside the data on still unpaid interest-bearing loans that can be found in postmortem investigations of sisters' assets. These usually (but not always) refer to "bonds" brought with the women as payment or dowry to enter the nunnery. (Perhaps the women had been moneylenders in lay life and gave up their profession; perhaps members of their families were bankers or moneylenders and gave the bonds to them.) Whatever the case, small payments were frequently required for women to enter conventual life; and bonds, for debts payable, were an asset that a potential sister could use to pay the fees. Or she might assign to the nunnery the interest on the bonds. Or, finally, she could promise to bequeath the bonds to the nunnery.

Much more interesting are the debts in these postmortems generated from interest-free loans (*prestato gratis*), suggesting that they were granted in the spirit of Christian charity, to "lend without any hope of return" (Luke 6.35: *mutuum date, nihil inde sperantes*)—from funds still under the authorization of the nuns while in the nunnery. For example, sisters could make no-interest loans (or authorize them) to other sisters who needed small amounts of extra money to obtain more comfortable or warmer rooms. At other times nuns lent (or, again, authorized the lending of) money to girls and women who needed small sums to pay the entrance fees for conventual life.[127] By doing so the lenders fulfilled Jesus' commandment and also nurtured the genial dependency or gratitude of the recipients. A few sisters must have begrudged the fact that their benefactresses had given them loans instead of gifts; a few probably begrudged having to be grateful at all. But the social world created by this kind of lending does not seem to have been one particularly ripe for recriminations.

A legitimate comparison might be made with the almost altruistic gestures of generosity from lenders that sometimes occurred among relatively well-born widows who lent small amounts of money or engaged in pawnbroking. There is no doubt that many of these women, as some English cases show, had been lending small amounts of money in their widowhood to close kin, perhaps especially but certainly not exclusively to other women and young people, without interest, to be neighborly or to maintain family solidarity and respectability. They gained nothing but gratitude and confirmation of their own virtue from doing so. Thus it is not surprising that many of these loans are known about precisely because they were forgiven in wills, the act of forgiveness being a further confirmation *in extremis* of the virtue of the benefactresses.[128] Perhaps the debtors had wanted to pay their debts or were in the process of doing so, but the approach of death stimulated in the widows what Rabelais called "Pantagruelism," after his hero, namely, the willingness to accept the desire to repay as repayment itself.[129]

These sorts of lending with, so far as altruism is possible, a deeply altruistic tint, were not rare. A more complicated illustration again involves nuns—those with shady backgrounds. In this case, certain men seem to have cadged loans of former lovers from among the hordes of reformed prostitutes who, in the wake of Franciscan and Dominican campaigns in Italy to rescue them from the streets and brothels, entered and ended their days in nunneries. Outstanding debts owed to these women at death include small interest-free loans to men.[130] It would be hard to assess the "psychological" stress that giving such a loan would entail, but some sublimation almost certainly occurred: here was the convert helping the still unconverted. Just as certain, however, was the mixture of disgust and nostalgia that went into the making of the loan and the fear, while the benefactress lived, that other sisters who found out might misinterpret her motives. As in the fictional representation of the dregs of port life in Algerian colonial society studied by David Prochaska, old lovers down on their luck and ne'er-do-wells keep turning up; pity and memories of different, even shameful times, yet times dappled with pleasure, made it hard to deny them a little money—whatever the risk to reputation.[131]

Pawning

The type of credit transaction, as opposed to environment, that most problematized women's social relations with one another and with men was pawning. The pledging of objects for money or other necessities is as old as the Bible.[132] It may be the most frequent species of credit transaction in pre-modern societies. Pawnbroking, the formal organization of such credit, went on everywhere in the world. There were 20,000 pawnshops in China alone in the late sixteenth century.[133] It should come as no shock, then, that most of the male and female moneylenders, Jews and Christians, who have come down to us in the records were pawnbrokers too, even if for favored customers they would occasionally make no-collateral loans. Customers for these people were frequently women, and again the evidence is well distributed across the map of medieval Europe: Catalonia and southern France from the Pyrenees to Provence,[134] the Holy Roman Empire,[135] and so on.[136] In the inventory of one (male) pawnbroker in northern France in 1394, of 813 pledges in his possession, 23 percent had come from women customers.[137]

To some extent we have already had the opportunity to consider the problem of the female borrower. She may have preferred to go to a female pawnbroker to avoid suspicions of having compromised her sexual virtue or because women specialized in handling "female" articles like kerchiefs and aprons.[138] But even when she did avoid male pawnbrokers, the potential remained for corrupting impulses to arise out of these transactions. For, although pawning may have been a routine experience in terms of the frequency of the exchange, it was not routine, if by this we mean innocuous, in its social implications. For one thing, it created at least an ephemeral sense of acute dependency in the borrower. Certainly, if the exchange was repeated—if the borrower, unable to redeem the desired pawn, returned habitually to pay the interest or found it necessary to pawn other objects—this sense of dependency hardened.

Dependency need not have generated humiliation. To be sure, relinquishing to a pawnbroker objects precious to the borrower could hardly have been a refreshing experience. Jewelry, fancy cups and plates, bedding, best clothes had to be parted with over and over again by indigent women. Their men gave up animals and tools as well, even the temporary loss of which made the possibility of the family's financial recovery all the more unlikely.[139] Most of the injunctions about pawning, as far back as the Bible, foresee the danger: "No one may take a mill or a millstone in pledge," decrees the author of Deuteronomy, "that would be to take life itself."[140] Yet there was never much concern on the part of authorities over the pawning of domestic articles.

By and large, one presumes, transactions involving domestic articles went "right," that is, lenders and borrowers settled on loans that both parties considered reasonable given the value of the objects pawned and that eventuated in the objects' redemption by the borrowers. At other times, however, transactions were less smooth and the results less happy. Sometimes the pledges were rejected. Sometimes they fetched far less than the customer needed or expected. Sometimes they were sold before the borrower had time to redeem them.[141] Nearly every instance of these sorts of botched transactions must have embittered the attitude of the borrower toward her pawnbroker.[142]

In part it is considerations like these that give force to the received wisdom among scholars who have studied the relationship of pawnbroker and borrower, namely, that a sense of *unjust* dependency on the part of the borrower was a frequent accompaniment and that a sense of disdain or haughtiness often infected the lender. Of course, such feelings could intrude on other credit relationships, because the extending of credit could easily give moneylenders leverage over the small productive resources of a homestead. Loans were readily conceived as a form of "earnest" money, advanced so that the borrowers were obligated to sell their crops, wool, wine, or whatever, when they became available, to the moneylender or give the moneylender a better deal or first choice. Looked at one way, this may be described as the creation of clientage, and may be beneficial to both parties. Looked at a different way, such transactions have more than a hint of manipulation about them, by creating obligations that place the producer at a disadvantage in the marketplace. Such dependency would also be unjust.[143]

Nevertheless, feelings of unjust dependency were much more common in pawning transactions of the classical type: pawnbrokers were not admired. Their crustiness, no doubt, owed a great deal to the very nature of pawnbroking in the Middle Ages. I believe that Raymond De Roover's picture of the medieval pawnbroker's business difficulties is overdrawn. But it is clear that there were annoyingly burdensome aspects to it. Some pledges, like grain, could spoil. Inventories could get very high, since Christian authorities prescribed long waiting periods before pledges could be sold. This in turn necessitated the leasing of additional space. These same authorities, who considered the periodic payments made by borrowers to pawnbrokers to keep the latter from acquiring the license to sell their pledges to be the most manifest usury, imposed unusually high taxes on pawnbrokers.[144] Police regulations were also meddlesome: snoops were always on the lookout for evidence of the fencing of stolen goods or of the acceptance of prohibited pawns (such as objects used in the Christian cult), often with good cause.[145] That pledges were even demanded from reliable borrowers whenever the moneylenders felt themselves at risk (say, from the possibility of expulsion or of the cancellation of their debts) added another ugly dimension to these relationships. But what should we expect? A moneylender who foresaw his exile was better off skipping town with as many objects as a pair of saddlebags would hold than with a thousand uncollectible promissory notes.[146] Men and women who dealt in pawns were often suspicious, and they must have shown it fairly often.

Pawning that involved domestic objects exacerbated the potential for nastiness, partly because those objects so often had a sentimental value to borrowers that transcended their intrinsic value. The dreariness of being offered still one more quilt, one more maple cup (or the same maple cup for the third or fourth time), must have played on the features of many pawnbrokers, with the inevitable resentments of the person in need. Moreover, these feelings were aggravated, on both sides, when there was a perceived class, racial, ethnic or religious barrier separating lender and borrower. When the borrower was from a group that was generally dominant in society, yet had to pawn with a lender whose race or religion she regarded as inferior, the feelings of humiliation took a nasty turn toward malice. On the other side, the lender's sense of dominance could easily transform itself into feelings of moral superiority and hubris—the manifestation of a latent desire to get even.

No single text from a period as distant as the Middle Ages is likely to make these points explicitly, but consider the case of the monks and nuns of Pavia who petitioned the duke of Milan on 10 May 1531 for permission to borrow from the Jews. They were reduced to this necessity, they lamented, because other factors made their poverty so great that they were going hungry. To secure the loan, they prayed the duke's permission to pawn otherwise prohibited ritual objects. Reluctantly or not, he agreed.[147] Securing the loan would have given them material sustenance; it could not have assuaged or effaced the memory of the degradation and the pollution they themselves permitted of Christian holy objects. Is it any wonder that within the next few years, groups of townspeople alleged that the Jews were levying extortionate interest; others raided Jewish pawnbroking establishments in Pavia; and others set out in various ways to make Pavia Jew-free?[148]

Although the negative emotional contours of the pawnbroker's relationship with the borrower are well known, it has been argued that there are strongly positive dimensions to the relationship as well, at least on the borrower's side. Going to a professional pawnbroker insured a good deal of secrecy. To seek a loan elsewhere, such as with close family members or neighbors, would have been in many cases an invitation for censure of the borrower's improvidence or waste: the classic case is that of the mother-in-law who berates her importunate daughter-in-law for her inability to manage the household. Humiliation does not require the crossing of confessional or ethnic lines. Recourse by a Christian woman to, in the paradigmatic case, a professional Jewish pawnbroker, who kept his or her mouth shut on business matters, preserved a level of privacy, limited only by the conspicuousness of the absence from the borrower's household of the article pawned.[149] To this extent, to borrow from a Jew or a member of some other out-group had a significant positive dimension that is difficult to measure or assess overall, but may be no less real. In any case, there are instances of what appear to be outstanding examples of positive relations between pariah-group moneylenders and their clients—though not prominently involving pawnbroking or domestic loans.[150]

In other words, one can find cases of Jews and Christians working together effectively and cordially. Occasionally they even joined together or fronted for one another in business enterprises.[151] But to generalize from these cases would be fatally wrong. I argued above that interest rates are not a good standard against which to measure the burden of a small short term loan, but they are good indicators of the relative ability of particular groups to attract business.[152] In the business of moneylending and pawnbroking, people who charge less do so because they are trying to attract customers who prefer to go elsewhere. They will in fact charge so much less that their own profits are small. This pattern appears everywhere in medieval Europe. Jews were forced to undersell Christian moneylenders, with catastrophic results to their profits: one calculation puts Christian charges at 60 percent to 80 percent of principal in the same region where Jews were lending at 20 percent to 25 percent.[153] Christians did not match them, because the profit margins on small, short term loans did not seem worth it. Christians could get away with charging higher interest, to the chagrin of authorities,[154] because the customers—other Christians—preferred to borrow from them. This conclusion has sometimes been denied or challenged: one researcher has suggested that minority lenders were just "less greedy"![155] But the point seems proved; indeed, the pattern of pariah-group lenders charging less than mainstream lenders is not unique to medieval Europe. The case of Ottoman Jerusalem in the seventeenth and eighteenth century may be compared: Jews attracted business by charging 8 percent; lenders from among the dominant Muslims charged 20 to 30 percent.[156]

A special case worth mentioning in any discussion of pawnbroking is that of Jewish "banks" set up in towns throughout Italy and the Avignonais. Despite the use of the word bank, these organizations were intended to provide cheap consumption and distress loans (at, say, a nominal interest charge of 5%) for indigent citizens or, in university towns, for impecunious students.[157] They were closely regulated and sometimes set up with difficulty owing to opposition.[158] Opponents favored *monti di pietà*, common funds underwritten by Christians to offer low-interest loans to the poor. The problem was in getting wealthy Christians to invest in these: some flourished, but many suffered or failed from undercapitalization.[159] Where there was an absence of effective Christian banks, Jewish pawn banks were established in Italy, increasingly in the fourteenth and fifteenth century.[160] Despite continuing clerical opposition they survived the Counter-Reformation as well. The requirement to serve the fiscal interests of the poor became in Pullan's words "a kind of *corvée*, a service owed [by the Jews] to people and state."[161]

The banks were ordinarily licensed by the papacy. Even when they were established outside the Papal States, the Jews themselves saw another source of protection in a papal concession/confirmation.[162] The banks came to be widely depended on: when a rumor flew in 1482 that the Jews of Pavia would no longer lend because they had too many unredeemed pawns, the *podestà* of the town feared riots if the rumor came to be widely believed.[163] This was rather different from the situation in Pavia half a century later when, because of their dealing in sacred objects, Jews became the target of popular forces that wanted to drive them from the town.[164]

In the vast collection of papal licenses and confirmations examined and catalogued by Loevinson in the 1930s, a large number established or renewed pawn banks with female heads. Many of these were widows who were continuing their husbands' banks;[165] others were daughters doing the same, probably, after their fathers' deaths or joining their capital with that of brothers or other relatives in order to perpetuate family businesses in the small loan market. To take merely one town, Ancona: from 1589 through 1669, 278 such licenses and confirmations were granted, of which 41 (approximately 15%) went to women or, much rarer, to tiny groups of two or three people of whom one or more were women.[166] A curious fact is that the proportion (15%) of loan banks placed formally under female control conforms closely with other fragmentary evidence on Ancona moneylending transactions carried out by women creditors (also 15%).[167] These are comforting statistics. They probably reflect a strong tendency among women to take an active role in these banks; they were not mere silent partners. Where they were prominent, they probably attracted female clientele. Unfortunately, the additional data to sustain this hypothesis are very sketchy: it must remain a supposition only.

Moreover, even if the supposition is true, it does not mean that the

networks of lending and borrowing thus created were conducive to sociability. There were towns in Europe where the activities of Jewish women
as moneylenders seem to have been looked on by Christian authorities as
unsavory and proscribed or, at least, curbed somewhat. Few Jewish women
were active in late medieval Montpellier or in Salon-de-Provence in the
fifteenth century; yet in both locations Christians—men *and women*—
and Jewish men were in the moneylending business.[168] That unsavory
impression might easily have been generated by disputes between women
of the two religions. There are just too many violent incidents between
Christian women and Jewish women in towns having or serviced by Jewish pawn banks, for instance, to allow rosy interpretations, as a perusal of
any major collection of documents demonstrates.[169] In 1452 there was talk
in the town of Cuneo, according to the record of one of these incidents,
of an expulsion order of the Jews, but no one knew when or if the order
would be carried out. In reaction to the Lenten sermons of a Franciscan
"on one day an unexpected riot broke out of women and children who
with stones *de facto* threw the Jews out of Cuneo."[170] Is it significant that
women and children took the lead in the riot? Or, better put, is it remotely
possible that it is not significant?

The Aristocratic Consumer

Almost all the transactions we have studied were not only short in term
but also small in size. Yet consumer credit was extended to aristocrats as
well as common people; and the consumption "needs" of the former far
outvalued those of the latter. It may seem anomalous to call the large loans
taken out by many aristocrats consumption loans, but the truth of the
matter is that most of them seem to have been so. The case of the Duc
de Berri helps highlight this issue and raises a number of important
points.[171] The duke's financial difficulties were notorious in the late fourteenth century. He mostly sought relief from "Lombards," Italian moneylenders in France who played a significant role in commerce and state
finance. Yet in March 1377 he was at his wits' end. Secretly, on two
occasions, five of the duke's closest collaborators went into the Jewish
quarter of Paris to visit a Jewish woman pawnbroker, the widow Précieuse
by name. These men included the master of the duke's household, his
chamberlain, his comptroller of expenses, his chancellor, and the count of
Sancerre (a close adviser).

They pawned a great many objects with Précieuse, who seems to have served as a broker or associate of a much larger group of Jewish moneylenders. The total series of loans came to the enormous sum at the time of 2,300 francs; yet the money did not go to productive purposes (say, to finance a mill on the duke's estates), but simply to support the extraordinary level of household expenses associated with his style of living. And if we have any doubts on this point, they vanish when other facts become known. The loans were given so short a term for repayment (only until 1 May) and charged so high a rate of interest (78%) that, if we did not know it from other sources, we could still conclude confidently that the loans were consumption loans. Given the size of the loans, however, the absolute amount of money demanded by the interest payments became unmanageable even over the short term—which was not a typical problem in consumption lending and borrowing. The duke could not meet the 1 May deadline. After paying 200 francs of interest, he still owed, on 1 February 1378, 972½ francs. His men managed to renegotiate downward to 600 francs.

Several things are revealing about this episode. First, and perhaps a bit startling, is the secrecy surrounding the duke's search for loans. We are wont to think of noble indebtedness as a given in late medieval and early modern times—nothing to be ashamed of. Perhaps this is a fair impression, and we know that the duke routinely purveyed on credit from victuallers, many of whom were women.[172] But this source had a limit: the solvency of the victualler. The kind of indebtedness that would drive a duke's highest counselors to a consortium of Jewish moneylenders headed by a pawnbrokeress was probably something that deserved to be hidden. It implied that preferred sources of credit (victuallers, merchants, even the Lombards) were unwilling to extend help and that the duke was brought so low as to pledge what, given the sums, were in fact priceless objects.

The case of the Duc de Berri also reminds us that with regard to large loans the market was different from that for ordinary consumption loans. If women had or could mobilize the resources to make large loans, they very likely made them to household stewards or servants[173] or directly to men or male-dominated institutions, not to other women. There must have been exceptions, but unlike the case with ordinary consumption loans, women-to-women networks are not consistently prominent.

One of the reasons the Duc de Berri was strapped for money was the financial demands put on him to marry his children well. Indeed, the number of large loans meant to help cover such costs among gentry, upper bourgeois, and aristocratic families was very high.[174] And it is hard to feel comfortable about classifying such loans as consumption loans. What is certain is that they were endemic. A particular cause of this was that the number of aristocratic men of marriageable age was frequently very low in relation to the number of aristocratic heiresses or widows with property. Men were constantly vulnerable to death in duels, civil wars (which seem to have been almost continuous), melee-like tournaments (at least, from the twelfth century), and foreign wars, including the Crusades. Women with rights in significant amounts of landed property vied for the protection (and love) of eligible husbands in what were virtually bidding wars. Most important to us, women appear to have advanced large sums of money in the form of loans to potential grooms; or, at least, so Jack Ravensdale has suggested in his study of late medieval Cambridgeshire.[175]

We may regard these advances as gifts; but it is not likely that any of them was reckoned as anything other than a loan, repayable to the woman's estate or to her family, until the marriage was successfully concluded. The potential husbands took out the loans for one major reason: it made good sense for them to secure the friendship and condescension of the heiresses' overlords by generous oblations that ostensibly came directly from the grooms-to-be. At base, customary law supported this practice with regard to aristocratic widows and heiresses who were "in their lords' gift" and needed permission to marry, but Ravensdale has referred to the practice as "selling . . . widows *dearly*" (my emphasis). Clearly the sums involved far exceeded customary requirements.[176] The ultimate disposition of the capital, of course, may have been for productive purposes.

In any case, the evidence of various types of loans (including long term purchases on credit) made to the elite for matters of consumption or related to "lifestyle" is relatively rich. It frequently comes from household accounts and testaments.[177] Kate Mertes's study of the English noble household from 1250 to 1600 brings together evidence of expenses "overwhelming receipts." Though claiming to distance herself from historians who think that the imbalance implies routine living on credit, she writes elsewhere that "many households suffered under a chronic shortage of cash" and "could, and distressingly often did, purvey on credit, building up huge debts which they were in no hurry to pay."[178]

A chronology of this form of noble and gentry indebtedness would locate examples across the entire range of medieval and early modern history, but there were periods when particular economic conjunctures exacerbated the situation. One such illustration is furnished by thirteenth-century England and France, where inflationary pressures undermined the wealth of a noble class that earned the largest portion of its income from fixed rents; another by sixteenth-century Scotland, where the relative inelasticity of income proved a handicap when demands for increased conspicuous spending and consumption at court were made of noblemen and women.[179]

Being a creditor to noble and gentry households at any time was both a bane and a godsend—a bane when the merchant had debts that he or she had to discharge, a godsend when it resulted in the merchant's monopoly over supply to the noble household. Why would a baronial steward go, cashless, elsewhere?[180] Moreover, what has been demonstrated for debt-clientage relationships in other pre-modern societies surely can be applied to the pre- and proto-capitalistic economy of medieval and early modern Europe, namely that "long patronage" of a merchant including, of course, occasional if fitful and partial payments of debts would lead to a culture of "bargains." The merchant would perhaps reduce already high interest (recall, again, that these were consumer loans, anomalous only in their size) or provide goods *under* market value to preferred (long term) debtors.[181]

As remarked earlier, in the medieval and early modern period stewards or servants often did the borrowing (the buying on credit) for gentry and noble households. Unfortunately, the vulnerability of merchants and lenders who extended credit to servants rather than to their masters was potentially severe. Undoubtedly the servants were bona fide agents of their masters in the universe of financial opinion. Whether they were so in the eyes of the law was another matter. We read in the *Register of the Privy Council of Scotland* of a widow in Edinburgh, precisely at the time when noble indebtedness was reaching crisis proportions in the late sixteenth century, who could not recover an extremely substantial debt of 266 pounds from

> a domestique servand with Johnne, Erll of Athoill, be quhome he is intertenyit, mantenit, and kepit in houshald with him, as man and servand, in sic sorte as the complenare can gett na executioun aganis him be letters of captious or uthirwayes.[182]

The good earl of Athol we know from other evidence was on the edge of bankruptcy when he sheltered himself from the widowed merchant behind the servant, as if such enormous debts were the servant's own.[183]

Nonetheless, despite all the problems incurred from lending to noble households or to stewards acting formally or informally for them, the practice was common. Moreover, there was one additional advantage that accrued to the creditor whenever a substantial portion of a noble's debts were, as they occasionally were, liquidated. The windfalls on these occasions to merchant households, thanks to the "forced savings," could be applied for productive purposes and fostered curiously strong affective feelings toward the debtor/patron. Becky Sharp, in *Vanity Fair*, brought torment to many merchants' and shopkeepers' lives and to the lives of her own servants, from whom she borrowed in the course of her marriage to Rawdon Crawley; but she also brought mirth and renewed trust those few times that she paid off substantial parts of her debts. Her fictional "story" is no different, in this regard, from the true stories of innumerable ladies and gentlemen of early modern Europe.[184]

Notes

1. Cf. Firth 1959, 39.
2. The difficulty of distinguishing credit from delayed gift exchange is immediately apparent from the discussions in Sahlins 1972, 185–275; Forde and Douglas 1967, 21; Firth 1965, 314–51; and Firth 1959, 422–32.
3. On Rome, below, pp. 14, 56.
4. Rostovtzeff 1941, I, 163; III, 1352 n. 37.
5. Rostovtzeff 1941, I, 404–6, 411; II, 672; III, 1418 nn. 202–3.
6. Rostovtzeff 1957, I, 16–17.
7. Rostovtzeff 1957, I, 180.
8. Below, pp. 53–56.
9. For Rostovtzeff's views, see Rostovtzeff 1957, I, 58, 153, 172, 180. For comprehensive, if ideologically loaded critiques, see Finley 1983, 73–75, 185–86; D'Arms 1981; and Austin and Vidal-Naquet 1977, 148–50, following Finley.
10. See especially Pirenne 1937, 1–3.
11. Postan 1927–1928, 236.
12. There are a number of classic works addressing the scholastic analysis of usury. Most of the discussion in the following paragraphs is drawn from these: Langholm 1984; Nelson 1969; Noonan 1957.
13. On *usura* in its various contexts, cf. Shatzmiller 1990, 67–70.
14. Baldwin 1970, I, 271: "the usurer sold something which belonged to God alone, . . . time, a divine gift to all men." Scholastics developed the parallel argument on knowledge this way: as a gift of God, knowledge, especially knowledge of God (theology), ought not to be vended. Teachers (churchmen) with benefices (whence they could live) should offer instruction as a free gift to their disciples. Other teachers might demand only that which was commensurate with their physi-

cal labor. There were, of course, enormous variations on this argument; see Baldwin 1970, I, 124–30.

15. See, e.g., Gerber 1981, 100–118, on Jewish and Coptic lending in the Ottoman Empire, and, more generally, Zenner 1991.

16. Cf. Shmuelevitz 1984, 57; Gerber 1981, 100–118; Jennings 1978, 225–93; Jennings 1973, 173–91.

17. Jordan 1989, 45.

18. Medieval records frequently record the status of borrowers, rarely the state of their health. So it is impossible to know what proportion of people seeking loans were sick and needed credit because they could not work. Presumably, seriously ill people had their relatives seek loans for them if the relatives themselves were incapable or unwilling to help them out directly. Yet a number of sick people must have tried to negotiate loans on their own. What was it like to deal with these people? Did creditors hesitate to lend when they expected borrowers to die? Or did they, in these "small worlds" of the Middle Ages, expect relatives of the deceased to make good on the loans without much pressure? What were the social repercussions for moneylenders who were perceived to be unwilling to lend to very sick people? For purely comparative purposes, one may consult the study of Robin Marsh (1983) on rural Colombia. Based on survey data, the author found that upwards of 60 percent(!) of the recipients of credit in this underdeveloped society seem to have been seriously ill at the time of or immediately before the taking of their loans. This is an astounding proportion and underscores the possibility that the medieval records, in being silent on the health of the borrowers, may be silent on one of the principal aspects of their lives affecting the social relations of credit.

19. Langmuir 1960, 207.

20. Shatzmiller 1990, 25–53.

21. Martin 1979, 131–41.

22. Little 1978, 42–57; Little 1971, 16–49.

23. Schilperoort 1933, 93–97; I owe this reference to Dr. John Logan.

24. On Europe, see Gampel 1989, 37; Jordan 1988, 54; Bowers 1983, 66–67; De Roover 1948, 127. For Islamic comparisons, see Faroqhi 1987, 152, 172; Udovitch 1967, 262.

25. Jeffrey 1981, 351–56.

26. Rubin 1987, 89; Le Goff 1986, 9–68, 83–99; cf. also Baldwin 1970, I, 270–311.

27. Rabelais [1955] (*Pantagruel*, bk. II, cap. 30).

28. Fossier 1988, 152, underestimates the amount of surviving data.

29. For example, Mayhew 1987, 121. See also the hasty and ill-considered remarks in Komlos and Landes 1991, 38.

30. The same problem has been noted in early modern court cases; see Haagen 1986, 72, 120.

31. Cf. Franklin 1986, 196.

32. See, e.g., McIntosh 1988, 562.

33. Jordan 1983, 149; Jordan 1979, 47–54; Jordan 1978, 42–44; Nahon 1969, 1121–48; Langmuir 1960, 203–39. See also Delisle 1969/1851, 195–99.

34. On Germany, see Jenks 1978, 309–55; on Provence, see Lavoie 1973, 202–4.

35. Rigg 1905–1972, for the most famous, the Exchequer of the Jews of England.

36. A few examples: Assis 1988, 18–20, and Emery 1959, for Catalonian territories. Coulet 1978, 79–104; Gasparri 1973–1974, 22–24; and Castellani 1972, 583–611, for Provence and neighboring lands.

37. Toch 1982, 499–550; Irsigler 1981, 122–62; Davis 1888; Loeb 1884, 161–96.

38. Tawney 1925, 17–30.

39. Cf. Jennings 1973, 173–80.

40. For medieval Europe, Jordan 1988, 41, and Leroy 1985, 73. Compare Faroqhi's observations on seventeenth-century Anatolia (Faroqhi 1984, 183, 281) and Skinner's on credit sales by itinerants in rural China (Skinner 1964, 30–31).

41. Shatzmiller 1990, 84–85; McIntosh 1988, 562; Bautier 1981, 217; Baldwin 1970, I, 300.

42. Holderness 1981, 195–209.

43. Shatzmiller 1990, 84; McIntosh 1988, 562.

44. Inn- and tavern keepers: McIntosh 1988, 565; Britnell 1986, 103. Craftsmen and notaries: Shatzmiller 1990, 84. Immigrants: Shatzmiller 1990, 89; Somers 1980, 118–25; Duby and Wallon 1975–1976, I, 524–26; Chomel 1951–1952, 225–47; De Roover 1948, 124, 148.

45. On the role of Cathar heretics, see Mundy 1982, 240, and Biget 1970, 1–50, but cf. Roach 1986, 54. For comparative purposes, see Crummey 1970, 135–57, on the role of the Old Believers in Russia.

46. Cf. Shatzmiller 1990, 91–93.

47. Shipley 1976, 467; Ashton 1960, 14–43.

48. Holderness 1984, 439; A. Clark 1982/1919, 28–29.

49. See, e.g., Hanawalt 1986, 151; Hilton 1975, 103.

50. Lacey 1985, 52; Wright 1985, 111.

51. Shahar 1983, 194; Wiesner [Wood] 1981, 4, 9, 12; Jacobsen 1983, 9; Riemer 1985, 61–62; Levy 1983, 210, but cf. Levin 1983, 161, 165, and Franklin 1985, 1–38.

52. Jordan 1988, 51; Noonan 1957, 73–75.

53. Below, see pp. 30–32.

54. E. Clark 1981, 262–63.

55. Nicholas 1985, 85–90.

56. Reyerson 1985, 67, 74.

57. The antiquity of the pattern is attested in Harris 1989, 148, who cites evidence from second millennium B.C. Mesopotamia.

58. Nicholas 1985, 85–90; Jacobsen 1983, 17–18; Clark 1981, 262–63. On the tendency of widows to maintain their husbands' businesses even in guild-strong societies like those of the Middle Ages and in traditionally male occupations, see Swanson 1989, 15, 35, 42–43, 74, 161.

59. Tallan 1991, 63–74; Baskin 1991, 45.

60. On occasional lenders, see Assis 1988, 34–35, including nn. 72–73, and below, pp. 36–38.

61. See, e.g., Assis 1988, 98–106.

62. Rigg 1905–1972, I, 89, 91, 106, 204, 208, 212, and so on, for primary references. For studies, see Lipman 1967, 47; Roth 1964, 115; Adler 1939, 17–18.

63. Jordan 1983, 149–50; Jordan 1978, 53. Cf. Powicke 1961, 213 n. 26.

64. Kohn 1982, 32.

65. Gasparri 1973–1974, 22–24.

66. Uitz 1986, 468.

67. Leroy 1985, 71–78.

68. Cf. Franklin 1986, 188.

69. Assis 1988, 29, 36–37; on Jewish men and their moneylending activities, pp. 50–58.

70. For an indication of the enormous bibliography on Italian Jewish settlements, see Braunstein 1987, 667 n. 4.

71. Simonsohn 1982–1986, I, nos. 47, 1196, 1561, 1630; II, no. 2042. See also Adelman 1991, 35; Stow and Stow 1986, 67; and Stow 1987, 1100—but Stow errs here when he says that Christian women were not involved as lenders.

72. Bonazzoli 1987, 750–51 n. 10.

73. Records from 1440, 1441, 1448, etc.: Segre 1986, 141 no. 318, 147–48 no. 329, 150 no. 333, 230–31 no. 491.

74. Bonetti 1982/1917, 40.

75. Simonsohn 1982–1986, II, no. 2201.

76. Simonsohn 1982–1986, II, no. 1697.

77. Some examples are noticed in Veinstein 1987, 802.

78. On the nature of Jewish businesses, including familial, and partnerships, see Assis 1988, 37–39, 45–48, and Jordan 1978, 42.

79. One such incident is recorded for a small Italian town in the sixteenth century in Segre 1986, 620 no. 1312. This is all that I have been able to find.

80. The comments of Professor David Berger, a Fellow of the Annenberg Research Institute at the time I was writing this part of the book, helped clarify my thoughts on this matter.

81. Northern France: Jordan 1983, 149–50; Jordan 1979, 47–54; Jordan 1978, 42–44, 53, 55. England: Lipman 1967, 47. Italy: Bonazzoli 1987, 750–51 n. 10; see also 751 n. 11 and 752 n. 21. Catalonia: Assis 1988, 36–37.

82. Below on borrowers, pp. 25, 29–32.

83. Shatzmiller 1990, 6, 74; Colafemmina 1989, 113–15; Assis 1988, 67–74; Kohn 1988, 86–88, 125; Reyerson 1985, 80–81; Kohn 1982, 38; Searle 1974, 402; Nahon 1969, 1135–36. Cf. Morenzoni 1992, 18–25.

84. See preceding note; also Assis 1988, 49; Mundill 1991, 163; and for useful remarks on rural credit, Wrightson and Levine 1979, 100–101.

85. Cf. Assis 1988, 83–86.

86. On the short terms of both kinds of loans, proceeding regionally, see: for England, McIntosh 1988, 561; Britnell 1986, 104; Searle 1974, 402; Elman 1939, 98. For France, Shatzmiller 1990, 6, 74; Kohn 1988, 86–88, 125; Reyerson 1985, 80–81; Kohn 1982, 38; Nahon 1969, 1135–36. For Central Europe, Samsonowicz 1988, 180; Jenks 1978, 331–32, 335–36. For the Iberian peninsula, Assis 1988, 67–74, 90; Leroy 1985, 63–65 (but cf. Gampel 1989, 38). And for Italy, Colafemmina 1989, 113–15; Stow 1981, 165; Poliakov 1977, 91; Noonan 1957, 34.

87. Above, pp. 18–19.

88. Britnell 1986, 104.

89. Below, pp. 36–38.

90. For some of the restrictions, see Dillard 1984, 90; Jordan 1979, 237; Pollock and Maitland 1898, I, 482–85.

91. Power 1975, 58. See also Morenzoni 1992, 11, for supporting documentary evidence from fourteenth-century Swiss Savoy.

92. Kohn 1982, 57; Kriegel 1979, 122–25; Shohet 1974/1931, 28.

93. Assis 1988, 60–62, 89; Leroy 1985, 71–78; Kohn 1982, 31; Shatzmiller 1982, 585; Richardson 1960, 116 (but cf. Dobson 1974, 14); Crémieux 1903, 246–47, 254–68; Cochard 1976/1895, 185–86.

94. Poliakov 1977, 18–20; Rosenthal 1962, 35–36.

95. Leroy 1985, 61, 72.

96. Kirschenbaum 1985, 270–89.

97. Cf. Shatzmiller 1990, 12, 21.

98. Kohn 1988, 246; see also Shatzmiller 1985, 330, and Kriegel 1979, 142.

99. Morenzoni 1992, 11; Brown 1989, 274; Assis 1988, 60; Dillard 1984, 90; Toch 1982, 512, 514–15; Clark 1981, 267–78; Irsigler 1981, 143, 145–46, 149–50, 152, 155; Jenks 1978, 332; Emery 1959, 64–65; etc.

100. Reyerson 1985, 77; Jordan 1983, 149; Jordan 1978, 45.

101. McIntosh 1986, 175; Riemer 1985, 71; Dillard 1984, 160; Jordan 1978, 53–55; Adler 1939, 28.

102. Britnell 1986, 104; Luzzatto 1902, 33.

103. Morenzoni 1992, 6; Jordan 1983, 145–46; Jordan 1978, 43–44; Clark 1981, 266; Hilton 1975, 47; Searle 1974, 402.

104. Cf. Britnell 1986, 104.

105. Jordan 1988, 36–37; Luzzatto 1902, 34–35.

106. For the figure on wages, see Jordan 1986, 63.

107. Above, pp. 23–24.

108. Shatzmiller 1990, 10, 116.

109. Cf. Assis 1988, 94.

110. Above, p. 24; see also Mundill 1991, 144.

111. Jordan 1988, 37–38. Cf. also for a Third World parallel Alexander and Alexander 1991, 383–84.

112. Cf. Clark 1981, 270.

113. Rabelais [1955] (*Pantagruel*, bk. III, cap. 4; see also cap. 3).

114. Erler and Kowaleski 1988, 7, 11.

115. Britnell 1986, 40–41.

116. Cf., for example, Lacey 1985, 51, on late medieval London, and Hutton 1985, 94–95, on fourteenth-century Shrewsbury.

117. Goldberg 1986, 29. On the shades of meaning and often the interchange-ability of the words huckster, forestaller, and regrater (reseller of goods bought at a different market), see Lacey 1985, 51.

118. Lacey 1985, 51; Hutton 1985, 94–95.

119. Britnell 1986, 40–41. Britnell draws on and, in part, quotes from the research of Hilton. Hilton has pushed these conclusions even further more re-

cently; Hilton 1992, 79–81. The social marginality of forestallers in medieval Denmark (women) and early modern Poland (Jewish) is attested in Jacobsen 1983, 11, and Hundert 1987, 259.

120. Hutton 1985, 94–95.

121. Faroqhi 1984, 6; Jennings 1975, 103; Jennings 1973, 194–97. Cf. Ulrich 1988, 83–86, for a situation that looks similar in early America; I owe this reference to Professor Michael Merrill.

122. The next several paragraphs restate and expand on some of my earlier views on this subject; Jordan 1988, 45–46.

123. For comparison only, see the wonderful field report of the anthropologist George Foster on informal moneylending among the women of Tzintzuntzan, a small Mexican village between Guadalajara and Acapulco, in the 1940s, which underscores the complex ramifications, positive and negative, of pawning, in this case, a flatiron. Sickness motivated the borrower to seek the loan to buy medicine. Her lack of respectability made the pledge necessary. She wanted more on the pledge than the pawnbrokeress was willing to give, but the latter had to dissemble about being cash-short to avoid recriminations. In the end, Foster calls moneylending "even between friends . . . a harsh affair"; Foster 1948, 144.

124. Cf. Assis 1988, 40–43.

125. Cf. Cassard 1984, 85–94, on Breton immigrants in medieval Paris.

126. The data may be consulted in McIntosh 1988, 562–70. I cannot say whether she would agree or disagree with the interpretation offered here.

127. Cohen 1985, 245, with additional information supplied to me directly by the author. Further on entrance fees, cf. Burton 1975, 21.

128. Holderness 1984, 439–41.

129. Rabelais [1955] (*Pantagruel*, bk. III, prologue).

130. The best treatment I know of all these issues is in Cohen 1985, especially pp. 245–47, but the discussion there is, as she readily admits, based on a small data base, very tentative and subject to revision. I want to thank her for access to additional unpublished data and for confiding her thoughts on these matters to me. Of course, my interpretation is not necessarily shared by Dr. Cohen.

131. Prochaska 1987, 13 (I want to thank Professor Prochaska for allowing me to refer to this unpublished paper, since his published work makes only passing reference to these issues; Prochaska 1990, 228–29). The risk to reputation, to pursue a point made in the text, might be greater if the supplicant were to be refused. Is there not a whiff of blackmail in these relationships?

132. See Deut. 24.6, 10–13.

133. Huang 1981, 144.

134. Reyerson 1985, 64; Castellani 1972, 605; Menkes 1971, 417–18; Emery 1959, 39, 49, 61, 64–65.

135. Toch 1982, 516; Jenks 1978, 335.

136. Above, pp. 29–30.

137. Kohn 1988, 138.

138. Cf. Wright 1985, 111.

139. On the types of objects pawned, cf. Jordan 1989, 62, 84; Assis 1988, 87, 90–93; Jacobsen 1983, 9.

140. Deut. 24.6; for medieval injunctions, Jordan 1989, 62, 84.

141. Lacey 1985, 52.

142. Cf. Jordan 1983, 149–50; Jordan 1978, 45–52.

143. Cf. Gampel 1989, 33–34, 125; Schwarzfuchs 1989, 224. Compare also Vassberg 1984, 207.

144. De Roover 1948, 128–29, 149, 156, 348. See also Poliakov 1977, 97–101; Gilchrist 1969, 72, 281 n. 141. Cf. the situation for modern pawnbrokers; Zenner 1991, 36.

145. Kohn 1988, 137; Wright 1985, 111; Kohn 1982, 42–43; Cohen 1980, 325–26.

146. Jordan 1983, 144–46, 150–51; Jordan 1979, 84–86; Jordan 1978, 52–53.

147. Simonsohn 1982–1986, II, no. 2434.

148. Simonsohn 1982–1986, II, nos. 2441–42, 2444–46, 2449, 2453.

149. Cf. Poliakov 1977, 48, 96; also Zenner 1991, 30.

150. Shatzmiller 1990; Shatzmiller 1989, 246–47; Cassuto 1918, 159.

151. Cf. Assis 1988, 40–43; Simonsohn 1982–1986, II, no. 3118.

152. Jordan 1983, 146.

153. See, e.g., Edwards 1988, 81–82; also Poliakov 1977, 57–62.

154. Cf. Assis 1988, 75–81.

155. Rosenthal 1962, 11.

156. Bashan 1989, 72.

157. Pullan 1987, 671; Simonsohn 1982–1986, I, no. 7. Special "common" funds for loans to students were known elsewhere: for medieval Cambridge, see Rubin 1987, 286–87; for Oxford, see Buck 1983, 106 n. 53.

158. Cf. Toaff 1983, 183–96.

159. The "idea" of the *monti* was not limited to Italy. It was "in the air" wherever the servicing of the market for distress loans raised moral questions; cf. Tawney 1925, 125.

160. Shatzmiller 1990, 84; Chiuppani 1979/1907.

161. Pullan 1987, 671; see also Ravid 1989, 206.

162. Loevinson 1932a, 3–4.

163. Simonsohn 1982–1986, II, no. 2089.

164. Above, p. 35.

165. See also Simonsohn 1982–1986, II, nos. 1763, 1903, 2361.

166. Loevinson 1932b, 28–46. Thanks to Loevinson 1932c, 167, and Loevinson 1933a, 59–60, we know that the phenomenon was not limited to Ancona, although the documentation is fairly rich for that place.

167. Above, p. 21.

168. Reyerson 1985, 73–74; Wernham 1979, 228–33. The question of social control is addressed, not on this issue precisely, but more generally in Jenks 1978, 335, 353–54.

169. For a few examples of female strife (Christian versus Jew): Savigliano in 1439, Cirie in 1440, Barge in 1469 and 1471, etc.; see Segre 1986, 136–39, 323, 329 nos. 306, 311, 719, 735.

170. Segre 1986, 255–56 note to no. 552.

171. The material on the Duc de Berri comes from Lehoux 1956, 50–52.

172. Lehoux 1956, 40.

173. Cf. Verdon 1986, 358, to the effect that gentlewomen rarely concerned themselves with household accounts.

174. Cf. below, Part Two, text to n. 89, on the *Monte delle doti*, which provided an alternative to upperclass borrowing.

175. Ravensdale 1984, 215.

176. Ravensdale 1984, 215.

177. Mertes 1988; Haagen 1986, 265. See also Tawney 1925, 31–42.

178. Mertes 1988, 77, 95.

179. For the English case, there is a debate; Carpenter 1980, 721–52. For the French case, see Jordan 1986, 28–32. And for Scotland, see Brown 1989, 266.

180. Mertes 1988, 112–13, 119.

181. Wharton 1962, 35; I owe this reference to Professor Walter Zenner. Cf. Shatzmiller 1990, 99–103.

182. Cited in Brown 1989, 270–71.

183. Brown 1989, 273.

184. Cf. Haagen 1986.

Part Two

Investment and Capital Formation in Late Medieval and Early Modern Europe

T he discussion of large consumption loans made to the high-born, which closed the first part of this study, is a fitting transition to a systematic consideration of the role of women in investment and capital formation. By these terms (and productive lending) economic historians denote the sorts of transactions, frequently involving large sums of money, whose purpose is the accumulation of resources for creating, sustaining, improving, or expanding farms and manufacturing enterprises or for making improvements in the infrastructure necessary for the marketing and transportation of produce and manufactured goods. Thus a productive loan might pay for deforesting a tract of land so that it could be converted into arable; for draining marshlands to the same end; for constructing and repairing barns; or for making fish weirs to improve the commercial catch on inland waterways. It might go to an artisan for raw materials needed for his enterprise or building the equipment necessary to set up shop. Productive loans also funded municipal investment to build bridges, improve roads, dredge waterways, build canals, and erect the walls and fortified towers which were needed at many periods for commerce to take place in peace.

Late medieval and early modern England and, as far as the scholarship indicates, continental Europe generally were the loci for some of the most active, complex, and well-documented networks of investment in pre-industrial times. They also witnessed a large volume of women and female associations acting in their own names and sometimes in distinctive ways (differentiated, that is, from the patterns of investment and borrowing of married and unmarried men and male institutions). All of which is not to say that similar phenomena did not exist in special or peculiar forms elsewhere and at other times. We may begin with Antiquity.

Antiquity

It may be presumptuous to entitle a subsection of this discussion of investment and capital formation, "Antiquity." The evidence is sparse and very idiosyncratic on men's roles in these matters, let alone on women's. Nevertheless, there are two or three points to be gleaned from the information that has survived, and this will at least lead us in certain useful directions later on. Let us begin with the work of Michael Rostovtzeff, who, as noted in Part One, had a very positive view of the extent and sophistication of credit in Antiquity.[1] Whether his assessment was correct with regard to consumer credit (and we have seen that there is some reason to doubt it), his principal interest was in investment, for which the evidence is a good deal richer. Some of this evidence, recovered or decoded only after Rostovtzeff's time, goes back to the period before Greek and Roman hegemony. Partial as it is, it gives us an indication of the role of women in providing the resources for capital improvements in ancient societies. And, not surprisingly, almost the earliest records relate to women affiliated with their husbands in business, who by necessity or choice exercised a myriad of functions that our stereotypes of ancient life do not envisage. Assyrian evidence from as distant a period as the nineteenth century B.C. provides information on women as textile producers for their husbands' businesses, as their husbands' agents during the latter's absence (though this role may have been informal), and even, in one case, as investor or creditor in textile manufacture.[2]

On occasion, institutions associated with the religious life of women in Antiquity became wealthy either through endowments or pious oblations and built up capital suitable for investment. Rivkah Harris has argued, from ancient Mesopotamian evidence of the second millennium B.C., that *nadītus*—celibate, frequently very wealthy women who dwelt apart from regular society in order to dedicate themselves to the cult of the gods— lived in such institutions. Unwilling to let their capital lie idle, the institutions served largely like banks, "concentrat(ing) their investments in . . . transactions such as lending money."[3]

The Greco-Roman world that Rostovtzeff studied has left additional evidence of investment and the social arrangements that surrounded it. "Investment banking" was *not* well developed in either Greece or Rome. Nevertheless, Rostovtzeff did manage to assemble data showing that in the fourth century B.C. loans for sea ventures ("bottomry" loans that canceled themselves on the loss of the ship) played a role, how significant being in doubt, in financing the trading operations of the Greek city states.[4] He also demonstrated that royal banking existed in Ptolemaic Egypt, although its importance and extent also appear impossible to determine.[5] There must, in general, have been a significant level of economic integration to sustain the subsidiary states of the great empires, the large cities, and the temple organizations of Antiquity. Even so, credit, according to recent scholars, remained embryonic and inadequate: not even Athenians had any really "big banks or wealthy [professional] moneylenders to turn to." The image instead is of traders "reduced" to scurrying about practically to cadge "money from miscellaneous people who had funds to invest."[6] Finally, although parts of the Hellenistic world, like Ptolemaic Egypt, did enjoy embryonic "systems" of credit that were capable at least occasionally of marshaling the necessary resources to help finance major building projects or the like, these did not undergo much significant development. They were stimulated somewhat to new sophistication under Roman pressure, if only because the conquered undertook to reconstruct their devastated cities and to pay tribute to the Empire,[7] but crushing taxation and bonded labor presumably obviated much of the need for credit. Elsewhere in the less developed parts of the Empire credit on the scale we are discussing was unheard of, despite the fact that the Roman presence proved a modest stimulus toward development.[8]

What do we know of the role of women in Greco-Roman investment? Only three women are mentioned on the *horoi*, the stone boundary markers used to signal debts or debt-ridden properties that have been studied by Finley.[9] None of the markers that mention women are Attic stones, that is, stones that would probably give us hints about the most elaborate forms of credit practiced in the Greek-speaking world of the time (500 B.C.– 200 B.C.). So the fact that only one of the stones names a woman as a creditor may reflect more on the underdeveloped nature of capital in general outside of Attica rather than on the precise role of women in the economy of golden-age Athens. Indeed, what the designation "creditor" may mean here is far from certain anyway.

Aristophanes provides some information for fourth-century B.C. Greece that suggests in fact that the minimal role of women in credit hinted at by the *horoi* material may, under certain circumstances, be misleading. In the *Thesmophoriazusae*, a comedy about women trying to obtain redress for the slurs of the poet Euripides, the playwright uses one scene to ridicule the demagogue, Hyperbolus's widowed mother, a war profiteer who "hoard[s] wealth, and lending monies, gather[s] profits far and wide." In Aristophanes's moral universe it was inappropriate for her to be seated at the public place of honor where he depicts her (and where, evidently, she was seated in the real events shadowed by the play). Emphatically she did not deserve a place next to Lamachus's mother, a *dis-*

tinguée whose son Aristophanes had steadily come to admire. Equally forceful is his insistence that her debtors should refuse to repay their loans.[10]

Much of the attack on Hyperbolus's mother is personal, for Aristophanes seems to have loathed her demagogic son. But it does suggest the remarkableness of women's (or a widow's) role in city-state finance in Athens, at least when war, with its disruption of effective taxation or its demands exceeding the return on taxation, gave them the opportunity to break whatever customary barriers to their activity existed. There is no doubt that those barriers did exist in Antiquity: Roman evidence, for example, reveals some women active as sponsors or investors in Roman trade in the region of the *Erythra Thalassa* (the borderlands of the Red Sea, Arabian Sea, and Persian Gulf) in the first century, but investment in trading enterprises was basically in the hands of freedmen.[11]

Yet, fragmentary, brittle, and exceptional as the evidence on women's involvement in investment in Antiquity is, it does, as I indicated at the outset, point to some fundamental features of the landscape that we ought to be on the lookout for as we pursue the theme into later times: the place of wives as business partners with their husbands, the potential for an active role for female organizations as foreshadowed in the sacred institutions that cloistered the *naditus*, the prominence of widows, and the uniquely empowering situation of war for wealthy women.

The Middle Ages and Early Modern Period: Background

Very little evidence has survived on credit transactions in the so-called "Dark Ages." Indeed, as we know, early scholars were unsure that an economy sufficiently sophisticated for systematic investment survived the collapse of the Roman Empire in the West.[12] The complex use of credit and credit instruments, in their opinion, was delayed until the Renaissance in Italy and until the Reformation period in northern Europe. Theirs was an exaggerated view, as Henri Pirenne, Michael Postan, and Robert Lopez long ago pointed out. The Flemish towns beloved of and studied by Pirenne had a well developed economy from the twelfth century onward, and the burghers were fully capable of understanding and using credit.[13] With a rich archival knowledge of English sources, Postan showed how the critics were consistently undervaluing the importance of productive credit elsewhere in the high and late Middle Ages, especially in England.

Although in his seminal work he did not discuss the market in credit instruments, attitudes toward credit and interest (usury), or the organizational structure of credit, he acknowledged their importance and their relevance to understanding medieval economic life.[14] Lopez concentrated for the most part on southern Europe. He favored the notion of the special role of Italy in what he called the "commercial revolution" of the Middle Ages, but he also saw elements of this revolution (frequently carried by Italians) in many parts of western Europe, such as in the economic life of the fairs of Champagne. Princely and municipal finances were dependent on sophisticated credit arrangements; and businessmen throughout the West engaged in a lively market in credit instruments despite increasingly strident criticisms, from the twelfth century, against mercantile activity and usury. Even churchmen who had to pay lip service to the criticism turned out to be some of the most astute businessmen and were not averse to benefiting from the fruits of "usury." Many certainly realized that access to credit made it possible for the institutions they headed, including the papal court, to enjoy a high level of financial stability and prosperity.[15]

This realization assuredly contributed to a more sophisticated view of the economic function of charging interest on investments than that developed in ecclesiastics' critique of distress loans. Interest on productive loans was not meant to purchase time but to reflect the level of risk undertaken by the creditor. There was no assurance, for example, that the voyage, on sea, by river, or on land, in which an investor put his hopes would ever be completed. The ship or barge could sink in a storm, be pillaged or sunk by pirates, find its expected cargo unavailable when it reached its destination, and so on. Caravaners could be waylaid. To encourage investment required the payment of interest. Without it, there would be no investment in trade at all, and towns—especially but not exclusively port towns—would be at risk of collapsing.[16] It was still not entirely congenial to many clerics to acknowledge the utility, let alone justice, of charging interest (and this explains at least in part the wonderful euphemisms that surrounded even these sorts of credit transactions),[17] but the system persisted and grew in sophistication.

It remained to be decided what was, even in this limited sense, the rate of legitimate interest, beyond which charges became sinful—usurious—even for productive loans: legal thinkers within the Church debated and debated this and similar problems.[18] As we shall see, the rates were low by current standards, and they were very low when compared to the (annualized) rates, 43.33 percent or 86.67 percent, usually permitted to

Jewish moneylenders for consumption loans. But low or not, it was hard to eradicate the shame of moneylending or of benefiting from moneylending even in the world of banking. The most arresting illustration of this fact, perhaps, is the evidence that has been amassed on the sensibilities of Jacob Fugger, the great early sixteenth-century German merchant banker, originally intended for a career in the Church but obliged by family responsibility to enter the family business. Not all the details of his involvement in the usury debate in the Germany of that time are yet known, but it appears that he and countless other well-born, wealthy, and urban oligarchs suffered much "private discontent" over their possibly usurious banking activities.[19]

Women and Investment

It is frequently said that a shift occurred away from the guilt-ridden culture of moneylending in the Middle Ages to a much more open acceptance of interest-bearing loans in the early modern period. Indeed, this purported shift has sometimes been signaled as one of the distinctive features of the transition to modernity. There is some truth to this, but the assertion needs qualification. Zealous antagonism continued against the "exploitation" of the poor who needed to borrow in distress. At the same time, in Protestant countries there was a strong ideological shift against private alms. The result was probably a continuation of pawnbroking and moneylending, whatever the misgiving, and a clandestine (and curtailed) level of informal giving to the poor. The documentary sources on poor relief show a growing number of widows in the early modern period demanding the welfare of the parish and of governments in general.[20]

Only with regard to productive loans do we find a noticeable ideological shift that tolerated, let alone encouraged, lending money at interest. As Norman Jones has recently argued, there was a growing public acceptance, first, of the economic *necessity* of interest-bearing loans (he dates this to around 1600), an acceptance that probably even penetrated rural areas to some extent; however, this was not immediately reflected in a change in what might be called the psychology of salvation. Men and women continued to suffer fits of conscience (or normative sources suggest that they should have), which their public activity would hardly lead us to expect.[21] Nonetheless, in the long run the dichotomy between conscience and public necessity worked in favor of a change in the former. By the mid-seventeenth century—and particularly with regard to productive loans—a major shift not only to the acceptance but also to the ethical legitimacy of charging interest had occurred.

Moreover, as Norman Jones notes, "moralists and legists" were much more given to justifying widows lending money at interest or investing in annuities precisely because they saw these as some of the few ways they could effectively maintain their livelihood (and, presumably, protect themselves from becoming wards of the parish).[22] Jones is describing the situation in northern Europe, especially England. Whether this attitudinal shift occurred much earlier in highly urbanized parts of the continent, like northern Italy, as has sometimes been suggested, is arguable.[23] What seems indisputable, however, is that the level of involvement, at least in any significant way, of women on the productive side of lending is earliest to document there. Evidence that has been accumulated for Genoa, Venice, Siena, and many other Italian cities establishes that women were already taking an active role in investment in the thirteenth century.[24] Not without its critics, the activity of women in the world of high finance nonetheless became commonplace in the Italian economy.[25]

Even elsewhere in Europe, where economic development and urbanization were far less advanced than in northern Italy and long before 1600, some women were active in productive lending. The place of Jewish women especially needs to be stressed here. Sometimes it is not possible to chart the nature of their investments, but the size of many loans granted by Jewish women in the high and late Middle Ages makes it clear that they were supporting much more than the habits of consumption of the *ordinary* Christian population. The evidence is spread across the map of Europe: England before the expulsion of 1290, northern French Jewish women in the fourteenth century, Jewish women throughout Provence, Jews of the Moselle, and so forth.[26]

It may be that the ease with which women involved themselves in productive lending and investments proper, which usually required a willingness to put a substantial amount of capital at risk, goes back to their involvement in consumption lending, particularly the kind to noble households that, we saw before, involved large sums or large credits.[27] However it originated, we encounter a quite astonishing amount of evidence for the late medieval and early modern period. Alice Clark's charming portraits of seventeenth-century English female capitalists, published early in this century, set scholars on the road to investigating this phenomenon.[28] Her impressionistic conclusion that widows (perhaps carrying on their husbands' businesses) were able to make a major contribution to capital formation has in some cases now been given statistical underpinning—and considerable nuancing, not to say deflating.[29] Nevertheless, widows, spinsters, and married women have been documented in important roles in a number of local studies: an investigation of early modern Wiltshire in England is one of these.[30] Another appears in an article based on wills and inventories from pre-industrial England, which sharpens some earlier work on East Anglia and Lancashire: in that article B. A. Holderness argues that the "most prominent economic function of the widow in English rural society between 1500 and 1900 was moneylending."[31]

Although because of its richness we will often focus on the English case, the prominent role of women in this regard has also been noted among the urban elites of early modern France in a recent article by James Collins.[32] And the same can be said about women and female institutions in several other European societies of roughly the same period.[33] Much of the discussion, therefore, will be comparative, and some attempt will be made to explore aspects of women's investment and lending activities that were unique to the continent or to Catholic regions of the south after the Protestant successes in the north.

Perhaps it does not need to be said, but the visibility of women in the role of substantial investors in late medieval and early modern Europe—Protestant or Catholic—compares favorably with that in contemporaneous Islamic countries. Undoubtedly, many credit transactions (certainly a greater percentage than in the European data) were hidden in societies such as the Islamic ones that bordered Europe and put strict controls on public or business activity by Muslim women. But among minority groups, too, in these societies the role of women in making productive loans seems decidedly muted. There is no doubt that some Jewish women were substantial moneylenders, in the sense of giving loans of large size, in the Islamic Middle Ages.[34] However, when for later periods, say, the early modern period of Ottoman domination, it becomes possible to reconstruct statistically accurate levels of involvement in productive lending, the place of Jewish women in the universe of finance capital seems very restrained indeed. They had a place: Eliezer Bashan recounts the transactions of one Bulla Ester, a shrewd Jewish woman trader in seventeenth-century Constantinople.[35] But according to Ronald Jennings the vast majority of productive loans, exceptions aside, were made by Turks (in the Turkish parts of the Empire); Jewish men were a decided minority of such lenders. Jewish women and other minority women are almost invisible—

in major transactions.[36] The European case may not be unique, but it is striking.

What, given their striking presence in investment, did European women invest in? Did their loans go for different purposes from those made by men? We shall see now that the answer to the second question is sometimes yes and sometimes no. Let us begin with the earlier Middle Ages and the evidence of large loans and long term credit, especially in the form of mortgages to freeholders in rural society. The money advanced was presumably used to improve existing properties or to clear new lands. One of the principal financiers or creditors—and the only one we know very much about (at least from a relatively early date)—was the Church. Lay lords undoubtedly exercised some of the same functions, but the documentation is not lavish. Jews were also involved, but precise evidence of the nature of their involvement is also relatively late.[37] Before the late eleventh and twelfth century gave rise to the intellectual and ideological revolution that would lead to a systematic critique of moneylending, it was clerics and ecclesiastical institutions (monasteries and nunneries) that constituted the major providers of credit.

The instances of ecclesiastical institutions providing mortgages are numerous. There was a great deal of pledging of land to churchmen in ninth-century Brittany, for example, which according to Wendy Davies "in many ways . . . looks as if they [the churchmen] were effectively operating as moneylenders."[38] Monasteries in Normandy down to and into the twelfth century and contemporary ecclesiastical establishments in and near Chartres routinely engaged in the same sort of activity.[39] Constance Berman has documented the activity of thirteenth-century Cistercian abbots in southwestern France in the mortgage market. Gerald Day has discovered evidence of the congregation of Savigny, a similarly constituted order noted, like the Cistercians, for its piety and austerity engaging in comparable practices in Brittany and Normandy in the thirteenth century.[40] Pirenne regarded the loans generated from the pledging of these properties as consumption loans,[41] but this seems a prejudiced, almost a frivolous opinion, stimulated by his desire to emphasize the creative possibilities of *urban* credit.

It has been suggested that nunneries, being on the whole less well off than monasteries, were less active in the mortgage market.[42] This is unquestionably true, but there is considerable evidence that their activity was far from negligible. Sometimes the nature of the sources is a problem, however. The language of gift and sale can obscure mortgages. The convent of Rinteln in the southern part of Germanophone Europe bought a number of pieces of property in the course of its history, but despite the language of purchase, occasionally we discover that these were conditional or redeemable sales, the equivalent of mortgages. One example, for instance, from the year 1277, has the seller, a knight named Ludwig Post, mortgaging a manse, a farmstead, and a serf to the nunnery for ten years.[43] Christina Vanja in an intensive study of the Cistercian nunneries of Caldern and Georgenberg and the Premonstratensian house of Hachborn in Hesse analyzed all of the charters that are known to survive from the convents. Scores of the transactions detailed in these charters seem to be sales (although they may cover up some mortgaging), but in a number of cases Vanja reads them explicitly as mortgages. Everything is mortgaged to the nuns: tithes, rents in cash and in kind, farmsteads, manses, meadows, gardens, odd acres.[44]

Despite papal disapproval, ecclesiastical institutions remained more active than many critics wanted right through the Middle Ages and, in Catholic areas, through the early modern period in providing productive loans. Vanja's data for Caldern nunnery extends from 1256 to 1525; for Georgenberg from 1252 to 1537; and for Hachborn from 1300 to about 1500. In Catholic parts of the New World, ecclesiastical institutions, parish organizations, and lay brotherhoods (confraternities) continued the practices.[45] Nunneries, not so "poor" here as in the Old World, became major lenders in colonial Mexico through mortgaging.[46] The evidence amassed indicates, as we might expect, that productive loans of whatever type made by these nunneries went to male members of the elite.[47]

What purpose did the mortgages per se serve? Ecclesiastical institutions were, of course, interested in seeing new clearances of land, and they were interested in cultivating local rural elites. Loans were a way of stimulating both. Presumably, most mortgages did not end in defaults or forfeiture. Many of the loans in Vanja's case studies can have had no other purpose than the creation of clientage.[48] A brazen attempt on any institution's part to encourage defaults or the concession of lands by freeholders in lieu of continued payments of the mortgages would have been recognized and resisted as an unfair practice, and would not have been conducive to good patron-client relations.

Actions and policies that were ruthlessly acquisitive and subversive of cordial relations might still have been advocated or engaged in by some profit-mad clerics, sometimes successfully, and this may partly explain later medieval *secular* legislation beginning in about the mid-thirteenth century aimed at forbidding alienation of lay property to the Church.[49] But even after this legislation appeared in many countries, ecclesiastical institutions continued to provide mortgages to freeholders, knowing full well that they could not acquire *dominium*, or ownership of the properties. The desire for influence rather than unalloyed greed explains the persistence of the practice.

The Cistercians make a good case for the inadequacy of property acquisition as a primary explanation for the extension of mortgages and direct credit of other sorts. In the first place, the heads of the order came down hard against any "usurious" practices; it did not take a great intellectual to fashion an argument that almost any mortgage could be construed as usurious. The Cistercians were dead set against becoming bankers, let alone bankrollers, and they repeatedly issued statements to that effect. One powerful one, for example, was issued in 1318, during the Great Famine in Europe, the worst natural catastrophe in medieval history excepting only the Black Death a generation later. At this time, the need to help freeholders and tenants was inducing many ecclesiastical institutions to lend money in one form or another and to guard against the risk of bad debts by charging what amounts to interest.[50] The year 1318, as famine conditions abated, was an appropriate point, then, for cautioning Cistercian houses not to persist in their "banking" activities. With nunneries whose disposable capital was relatively small in comparison with monasteries, the warning was probably effective. The data on Caldern and Georgenberg in Hesse, for example, indicate a marked decline in mortgaging in the fourteenth century: there is no greater number of mortgages recorded in the fourteenth century than in the thirteenth despite the enormous improvement in the data base; yet at least twice as many are recorded in the fifteenth century.[51] The Cistercian prohibition, coupled with the overall economic difficulties of the century on houses that, like nunneries, had very limited estates, could account for this.

Nonetheless, Brian McGuire has drawn attention to the activities of the male houses of the Cistercians (Denmark is his illustration) in just this period, which had little choice but to ignore the warning or be accused of being indifferent to suffering. For in many places like Denmark agricultural recession continued through the 1320s and 1330s (long after the famine had relented elsewhere, but before the Plague wreaked further havoc on the rural economy). Mortgaging of property to the Cistercians became common. Many of these mortgages did end in defaults, but at the time they were granted no one thought that they would. Rather, they were designed to help independent farmers, freeholders, weather an agricultural catastrophe unparalleled to that time. In the event, that catastrophe was too wrenching and too persistent to permit recovery within the parameters of the old agricultural regime. Independent farmers were transformed into tenants, not in a conscious policy to bring them low, but in hopes of providing them with some protection by association with institutions, like monasteries, that offered a prospect of survival. The Danish Cistercians, like some other orders, surely benefited in the long run from the transition, but it must have been a frightening gamble in the 1320s and 1330s.[52]

The Church's role as creditor was paralleled by its role as a very heavy borrower. Drought or excess rains that reduced crops and therefore food and (often) income for the religious community; wartime situations where priests, monks, and nuns endured the destruction of their property; major repairs to churches and other ecclesiastical buildings; the construction of new churches; onerous taxes levied on clergy either by princes or by other churchmen—all required money. Heavy borrowing was a response.[53] One roundabout method was to encourage direct investment in ecclesiastical properties in exchange for annual returns in the form of either cash or maintenance, or both. An investor (corrodary in the jargon) would invest a certain amount of money (perhaps a large inheritance or substantial life savings) in return for receiving every year food, lodging, and other considerations equivalent to some portion of that amount (the rates varied, but not very much). These investment-annuity contracts (corrodies) were especially attractive to people who were physically past their prime. Yet dependence on corrodies threatened not only to turn the ecclesiastical houses into nursing and rest homes, but also, in the absence of actuarial knowledge, into fiscally unstable institutions.[54]

Nunneries, which already had fewer resources than male institutions, were especially vulnerable. Some, in regions where Jews continued to reside, borrowed directly from Jews.[55] John Tillotson's study of the Benedictine priory of Marrick in north Yorkshire, where there were no Jews, at the turn of the fifteenth century provides evidence of that house managing to balance its accounts with gifts and loans from the local elite. In good times, the nuns lent money and accounted the return (or interest) under the heading "Alms," a neat way to euphemize.[56] The fragmentary fiscal accounts of the nunnery that reveal this also show that at other times it was the sisters who needed to borrow. After all, there were the expenses for the new barn, and for upkeep and repairs to several other buildings (a stable, two houses owned by the priory, a garden wall): this meant the payment of wages to carpenters, roofers, and masons. Farm equipment of various types—wagons, barrels, spades, plows, scythes—also went in for repairs or had to be replaced. The accounts have a special section on "Cost of iron" in the form of unfinished pig and specialized pieces, such as nails, specialty nails, horseshoes, plowshares, and supports.[57] The accounts reveal that men as well as women were called on to provide some of the loans;[58] but, supplementing this evidence with that of testamentary bequests, Tillotson concludes that "the ladies of the Yorkshire gentry had a particular inclination . . . to support these houses and individual nuns with gifts."[59]

Other nunneries, as intimated, went the route of establishing corrodies or even attracting municipal investment in return for annuities. The Poor Clares of Nuremberg appear to have done this or, at least, to have been fairly active in the annuities market.[60] The Benedictine nuns of Frauenalb aggressively pursued similar practices in the sixteenth century. The house managed to attract some substantial investments for an annual return that contractually seems never to have varied from 4 percent or 5 percent to the investor.[61] The 5 percent rate of return appears to have been fairly common at this time for a highly varied set of investments in German-speaking and German-influenced regions.[62] The magnificent data assembled by Vanja on the Premonstratensian convent of Hachborn, already referred to, reveal that house paying a number of "life rents" during the fourteenth century, some of which were presumably negotiated because of the bleak economic conditions that developed over the course of the century.[63] And Thiriot, writing in the early part of this century, discovered rather extensive material on the activities of the Carmelites of Metz in this regard. Some portraits of the corrodaries (or benefactresses, as the author preferred to designate them) are worth recalling here.

Marguerite Aubert, one of the benefactresses, had a family connection with the house. On 17 November 1681 she concluded a contract establishing the corrody. All the property in her gift was to go to the Carmelites as an endowment. In return, she was to receive a room, the promise of a dignified burial, annual prayers for her soul after her death, and an annuity of 500 francs of Metz money (a tidy *haut bourgeois* sum). When she died, however, members of her lineage sued. Nunneries in general did not have the resources to pursue their rights with the vigor litigation demanded in the late medieval and early modern period. The nuns preferred to settle out of court. They virtually ceded the principal of the investment (having benefited from the surplus income during Marguerite's lifetime), but they also promised to continue to remember her in their prayers.[64]

Marie Souplet became a benefactress in 1671. Her sister had long been a Carmelite in the house at Metz, but Marie, having married, had chosen a different career. When her husband died she decided the nunnery might be appropriate for her, but at age seventy was unsure. She opted for a corrody. It might be permanent or temporary, that is, until she decided to leave or to take her vows. She was very generous. She offered 1,000 pounds as an altar gift or endowment, 14,000 pounds at the free disposition of the nuns, and another 8,000 pounds as an entrance gift for a cousin who wanted to join the order. For her 23,000 pounds she received all the niceties, including the services of her cousin as permanent attendant and an annuity of 900 pounds.[65] The amount of the annuity is mentioned in the context of what she would receive if she left the nunnery. So it is possible that she received slightly less as long as she had the services of her cousin as a servant. However that may be, computed against the entire 23,000 pounds an annuity of 900 pounds was 3.5 percent. This may seem low, but similar rates are recoverable on other annuities involving substantial investments.[66] On the other hand, when computed—possibly more properly—against the 14,000 pounds, the rate of return negotiated by Marie Souplet was 6.4 percent. If this reckoning is the true one, the rate falls comfortably between the 4 to 5 percent calculated by Franziska Geiges for Kloster Frauenalb and the 10 percent return the nuns of Kloster Bildhausen were willing to pay in the early fourteenth century.[67]

In Protestant countries investment in nunneries became impossible, and the ability of old people to find a comfortable niche for their declining years grew more difficult. There is evidence that some less wealthy among the aged (women have the slight edge in the examples known) practiced a parallel form of securing their comfort by transferring their property early to their child or children in return for an annual contribution to their maintenance and the promise of nursing in their last illness. When we have evidence of formal contracts establishing these agreements, they usually have conditions: the elderly parent(s) would recover full *dominium* if the child or children became negligent in their responsibilities. The possibility of family strife and perhaps the certainty that the mature parent would interfere in the administration of the family property regardless of whether he or she had formally "retired" may explain why this particular form of annuity was rare. Yet, though relatively rare as a practice (or so a recent study of annuities in Württemberg would suggest), the existence of this method of providing for personal security underscores the broader vulnerability of aged widows in society and the pressures that would lead them to invest proportions of their fortunes sometimes far in excess of men's.[68]

What can be said about the other investment interests of women? Holderness describes the characteristics of 620 widows drawn from a sample of moneylending women in early modern East Anglia and Lancashire, most of whom were not professionals, but women left with substantial investible capital on the deaths of their husbands. Between 10 and 15 percent "of specific contracts of debts were mortgages." Provisional findings are that "the proportion of the principal which was lent upon mortgage amounted to at least one-third, and probably to about two-fifths, by value of the total sum." Such women also "spread risks" as men did by diversifying their investment portfolios, but being more dependent on this form of income than men, they tended to have a greater percentage of their resources out at loan at any one time.[69]

In contemporary northeastern Lancashire, according to John Swain's reconstruction, the situation seems very similar: "women (predominantly widows)," he writes, "had a relatively large amount of their assets as credits," that is, as money owed them at their demise. Although husbandmen had a similar proportion, "yeomen and gentry had just 19% and 10% respectively of their assets as credits."[70] Swain, well aware that not all credits were the result of investments, moneylending, or the extension of delayed payment on purchases, nonetheless seems confident that a great many of these "credits" were loans pure and simple. Moreover, the mean value of each credit in a woman's case exceeded the mean for all other computable groups: gentry, yeomen, husbandmen, clothmakers, tradesmen. An average credit listed as an asset for a woman was 47 percent larger than that for a husbandman, its nearest competitor, and a whopping 229 percent greater than that for a tradesman. He concludes that the "small number and high mean valuation of women's credits suggests that they were more concerned with lending larger sums of money, and hence probably at interest."[71]

L. A. Clarkson, considering evidence from Devonshire during the sixteenth and seventeenth centuries, discovered that there, too, widows lent money as "extensively" as the most active occupational group, merchants. He also discovered that the size of the portions that they put out at loan was "considerable." Debts payable constituted, moreover, almost one-third of "the total value of widows' estates worth more than £75."[72]

Again the implication is almost too clear: women with substantial investment potential were investing substantially; and they were doing so in average amounts that usually exceeded investments by men. Unable, on many occasions, either by age or inclination, to use their money for any other purpose, and yet by the peculiarities of English law having considerable say in the free disposition of their movable property and the issue of their lands,[73] they were helping to finance rural development in general in the early modern period.

To be sure, not everywhere were widows treated the same. Custom differed at the peasant level. Most peasant widows would not enter our data anyway, since our present interest is in large loans. But there were some rich peasants. When they lived under archaic manorial customs they frequently retained a strong interest ("freebench") in the land that their husbands had held, but this interest did not usually translate into much "free enterprise." It was enough—and it was safe—to exploit the land as they had always done. Where, however, these archaic customs broke down, free enterprise was possible. In a genuinely stunning study of villages in the Vale of Oxford, Barbara Todd shows the two processes at work: the conservatism of the freebench regime and the enterprise of widows outside the regime (in the so-called open village) around 1600. She highlights particularly how rich widows in the latter invested in real estate (lent money through mortgages) and in local traditional industries, like malting. Not everybody did well; that is the risk of enterprise. Nonetheless, "whether successfully or unsuccessfully, all these women were moving with some confidence in a credit market in the interests of themselves and their families."[74]

Most of the investments we have been discussing involve rural widows putting their money into real estate and, either directly or indirectly, into rural maintenance and improvement of agricultural production. Like the case of the benefactresses of the medieval Priory of Marrick, whose grants went to the purchase of iron and the payment of wages to keep up the physical plant, so, too, widows like Isabel Barlow of the still quite small Elizabethan town of Manchester (not quite the "greatest meer village in England," as Defoe would call it) provided credit to shoe, it would seem, nearly every horse and ox involved in agricultural production, carting, or mercantile activity.[75] T. S. Willan suggests that the extraordinary extension of credit documented here may be related to Isabel's husband's way of doing business. Possibly. But if so, she maintained it with great determination. He died in 1587; she was in business alone for seven years after his demise. And these loans/credits are recorded at the very end of the period.[76] In light of what is known from Holderness's, Swain's, and Clarkson's studies on the propensity of widows to accumulate "credits as assets," it seems more reasonable to interpret this as an acceptably female (or widow's) way to create clientage.

There is, indeed, a conservative aspect to this kind of lending, which concentrates on real estate, on sustaining traditional modes of production, and on securing maintenance for old age. We should expect this to be the case. Widows and spinsters (and orphans), to repeat a point made earlier, were dangerously vulnerable: this is one of the reasons that strong arguments were made about their *right* to lend money at interest in the early modern period. And the powerful persuasiveness of the arguments made on behalf of this "tearful orchestra" is borne out, as we have seen, by the escalation of widows' places on poor relief rolls.[77]

The behavior of some women in England with disposable capital was certainly different, showing perhaps greater willingness to take risks. No statistical underpinning can be given to this possibility. Like Alice Clark, who pioneered the field, to pursue the issue we would have to employ a biographical approach. Unlike her, however, we cannot use every indication of interest in finance or the household by a high-born woman as evidence that the woman was a "capitalist." When the exaggerations and misleading inferences in Clark's own study are winnowed out, we are left with very few portraits of risk-taking English women investors: shipping appears to have attracted the money of a few early modern widows (there was always a demand for any kind of private investors, at least until banking developed).[78] But examples like this *seem* exceptional. Whether they actually are depends on further research.[79]

On the continent there are great similarities to the situation in England. The prominent role of widows investing in mortgages, for example, has been noticed by Sabean for late eighteenth-century and early nineteenth-century Württemberg.[80] And we have already seen how relatively safe investments, like corrodies, may be found in the records of many continental nunneries.[81] But particularly for urban society the continental picture is more interesting. Italy probably offers the most sustained evidence of the volume and conceptual importance of female investment during the late medieval and early modern period.[82] Scholars have shown from thirteenth-century Genoese records that almost one-quarter of commercial (investment) contracts for trade involved women.[83] To be sure, women contributed less in absolute sums to the investment pool than their share of the overall number of investments would indicate, a fact that means that average per capita investment by women in trade was less than that by men.[84] But their role, as we shall see, was very significant nonetheless.

Because married women in Genoa could legally use their property to profitable advantage, the "overwhelming number" of cases of women investors is not comprised of widows, although in one study they do make up a substantial 26 percent. Even if in absolute terms women invested less than men on average, wives, per capita, could put out a larger *proportion* of their fortunes in commercial investment than husbands could, because they were not ordinarily encumbered with the other financial responsibilities of husbands. "From the size of their investments," one scholar concludes, "it is evident that Genoese women were important to the process of capital formation that provided the life's blood of Genoese trade. Genoese commerce would have been severely handicapped had their money been diverted to more secure forms of investment" like real estate and (neighborly) consumption lending.[85]

Although urban Italian women invested in these less risky forms of business, it is significant that their social vulnerability did not balance itself with economic conservatism. That is, they (or, more likely perhaps, the men who handled their investments) placed their money in secure forms of investment much less frequently than we might have expected. Clearly, other forces, including the desire of "investment counsellors" for spectacular profits (from which they would cream off spectacular commissions), pushed women who might well have preferred less risky investments to establish patterns of investment that at first sight seem counterintuitive. (The contrast with England is profound. There, as we saw, widows had considerable authority directly over the disposition of their capital.) The risk-taking that Genoese women were drawn into benefited for Genoa as a whole by diversifying its economic interests.

Work on other late medieval and early modern Italian cities is beginning to show similar sorts of behavior. The old orthodoxy that women, if they invested at all, always invested in risk-free enterprises or chose merely to spend down their capital on clothes and luxury goods seems untenable. In Venice, for example, we are only just beginning to recognize the distinctive patterns of female investment and to acknowledge that women's disposable resources were put into other than consumables.[86]

The capacity of Italian urban women, with the help of counselors, to use their capital in creative ways sometimes provoked a backlash. Work on

Siena alerts us to this fact. At the beginning of the thirteenth century, women in Siena had extensive though still limited property rights, particularly with regard to their dowries. Eleanor Riemer demonstrates that they took "advantage of the opportunities" afforded by economic growth in Italy "in ways that threatened male economic and lineal interests." In this case the "threat" had nothing to do with the various commercial foci of the investments but the tendency of women—or, at least, of some women—to enter commercial fields that put their fortunes at risk of devolving onto or dissipating into the hands of people outside the lineage. This provoked a reaction, namely, progressively greater limits on women's control of their capital.[87]

Besides trade, municipalities themselves offered an investment opportunity to women. Less risky than trade, they were still more risky than real estate or perhaps nunneries. Municipal finances were frequently in disarray in peaceful times, and city-states were particularly vulnerable in wartime. Direct taxation was always unpopular, so it was usual for municipalities to raise money in other ways. Some were bizarre. It was not unknown for municipalities with really pressing "cash-flow" problems to borrow money from pawnbrokers on the security of articles that belonged to the towns or over which administrators had leverage. Gold chains and other insignia of municipal office and dignity, cloth, and even church bells and cathedral plate were pledged by town councils, sometimes illegally (in the case of ecclesiastical objects) to Jews.[88]

Some of the ways are more familiar: indirect taxation, gracious gifts coerced from churches, special levies or forced loans from aliens or Jews, and the sale of what amounts to municipal bonds. Indeed, the typical contribution of a woman to the municipal treasury came in the form of investment in interest-producing bonds. In return for a large infusion of capital, municipalities promised annual (semi-annual or thrice-annual) payments calculated at some fixed percentage of the original investment for a term of years or for life (life rents). Unlike the corrodies in monasteries and nunneries, there were usually no maintenance provisions. The interest payments on municipal investments provided older women and widows (who may or may not have been the original investors) with pensions and younger women whose fathers or families made the arrangements with annuities or dowries. The famous (or infamous) *Monte delle doti* of Florence immediately comes to mind.[89]

Set up originally as an exigency of wartime finance, the *Monte* became a crucial element of the Florentine municipal financial structure. Its avowed purpose (in addition to raising money for the Florentine state) was to encourage citizens to buy shares, the shares (plus a certain rate of interest) becoming payable, upon marriage, to the husband of the girl for whom the investment was made. Shares came to maturity at various fixed times, and interest varied according to term. Elaborate calculations, not of great actuarial confidence, and a number of special restrictions (for example, the forfeiture to the state, under certain circumstances, of shares that could not be paid out at maturity) were meant to keep the fund solvent. Overly high interest rates and other problems periodically weakened the utility of the fund, but further investment could be encouraged to service the debt. One point that is germane to our concerns: in the case of the *Monte*, at least during its early history, the investors in general were men or families, the recipients men. Women benefited directly from the assurance of dowries to establish them in honorable marriages; they benefited indirectly from the added resources that their husbands commanded in their own business affairs.

Some northern French towns engaged in widespread encouragement of investment in municipal funds. But in the absence of a so-called dotal regime as was characteristic of Mediterranean societies, the return promised was typically only annuities and the almost preferred customer/investor was a wealthy widow. Some of these towns seem to have come close to bankruptcy because of the practice. In the absence, again, of reliable actuarial tables the *rentes*, or interest on the investments, could soon outvalue regular income. So new investments were encouraged both to service the debt and to make the needed capital improvements: covered markets, bridges, wharves, warehouses, town halls. This might have gone on indefinitely, except that northern French towns were anything but independent. Debt financing by municipalities was a practice that the royal government was sometimes hostile to in the Middle Ages; engaging in it could be grounds for the government to take a town administration into receivership.[90]

If the medieval French state was hostile to these practices, its early modern counterpart was not. Municipal bonds were tolerated, and, James Collins notes, "rich women, usually widows, played a key role in French capital markets" through their investments in these bonds. Women (or, rather, widows) differed from men in that a far larger proportion of their portfolios was directed into municipal and royal *rentes* because, Collins continues, "one of the chief forms of investment in seventeenth-century

France, office holding [that is, purchase of offices with income from their perquisites], was closed to women." Consequently, some towns were literally living from the investments of women, with, in one example, 20 percent of all municipal debts in the hands of women. (This very likely means that the majority of all investment came from women, for many of the debts owed to men could not have been *rentes*.) In another case, 55 percent of all investors were women, the reward for their confidence in local government being the interest that was returned to them as life annuities.[91]

As the national state took ever more relentlessly to debt financing in the sixteenth century, investment in royal *rentes* became an increasingly selected part of a widow's portfolio. Investments in Brittany have been particularly well-studied. They reveal that in Nantes, for example, women (alone or in groups) who are known to have purchased royal *rentes* constituted 33 percent of all purchasers. "The pattern," Collins writes,

> was everywhere the same in Brittany: at Quimper, in 1569, women bought 28.1 percent of the large denomination [royal] *rentes*; at Tréguier, the largest rentier was Coustance La Gadec (capital of 2,400 livres), and other women bought at least 13.7 percent and 20.7 percent of the *rentes* in 1570 and 1571, respectively; at Rennes, the second largest rentier was Janne du Breil (2,020 livres); at Vannes, one widow put up 2,592 livres in 1569, and four of the nine largest *rentes* of 1571 were bought by women.[92]

To the unsuspecting it may seem quite surprising that women were providing so much of the revenue to the French crown and probably even more, proportionately, to the towns. One reason for this, besides their exclusion from buying offices, was that there was a strong prejudice, based in reputation, against men capitalizing their wealth and granting away large amounts of it for a comfortable annuity to the disinheritance, as it were, of their families. It was much more acceptable for a widow, who had absolute control of only part of the property and who may have been very old, to purchase an annuity. This prejudice, however, had its limits. At the level of royal finance, men invested heavily in *rentes*, partly because doing so gave them leverage with important people in government.[93]

The national government was also usually hard-pressed for money and would seek it anywhere and everywhere. Widows were fair game. Annuities at 4 percent or 5 percent were probably not dangerous if they were granted to mature persons, if they were limited in term, or if their payment amortized the capital. The problem was that unlike most municipalities in France (and, as we have seen, in Italy and, for that matter, nearly everywhere else in Europe), the royal government was particularly inept in assuring against its own bankruptcy. The incessant demands of war—and the concomitant need for money—encouraged ministers to improve the return to potential investors to 10 percent. It persuaded them to abandon schedules based on age. And it convinced them to discontinue amortization, that is, the practice of charging part of the annuity against the capital invested, so that the annuity would run down in a set number of years. These modifications certainly did attract investors, the most notorious of whom were the so-called Genevan Immortals.[94]

By the eighteenth century French royal finances were in a terrible state. Unwilling to reconstruct the tax system radically, the government continued to float loans in the ways described above. As France's international commitments expanded, ever greater investments had to be encouraged. In the latter part of the century, certain citizens of Geneva, a city under French domination, came to the realization that, with their access to the government, they could exploit the situation. A 10 percent return on investments was good, but it would be better if the beneficiary of the annuity lived for a long, long time. Exploiting a quirk in French practice, which allowed a purchaser to name a "head," or person to whom the annuity was to be paid, a syndicate was formed (and later many others were formed) that invested on the heads of thirty women.[95]

Or, rather, girls. The Genevans chose girls. It was unwise, after all, to choose boys, who had a distressing habit of going off to war and dying at a young age. Besides, even though actuarial science was in its infancy in the late eighteenth century, it was common knowledge that more women than men lived to a ripe old age. So the Genevans chose girls—and they chose them carefully. The girls had to be in good health and somewhere between the ages, preferably, of two and seven. They had to have already had and survived dangerous childhood diseases. They were recruited from aristocratic and *haut bourgeois* families, so there was no danger that poverty might undermine their access to food or routine care and thus shorten their lives. The syndicate checked the birth and death records of their families so as to determine whether they came from long-lived progenitors. It is unlikely that as Protestants the syndicate actively discouraged the girls from marrying (to avoid death in childbirth), but they could not have been disappointed if some remained unwed. After this careful scrutiny the syndicate bought a French royal *rente* for each of the girls. The syndicate's best estimate was that no more than one of the thirty, on average, would die in each three-year period from the purchase of the *rentes*.[96]

It was a splendid success for the syndicate, for Geneva, and for the girls. Money poured in for the girls and was distributed as shares to the syndicate. Indirectly the girls benefited from this whenever their own family members were substantial shareholders. The girls also benefited from some of the most solicitous care ever lavished on a group of human beings in the history of the West. Every cough was immediately attended to. They were nursed, pampered, protected—perhaps, occasionally, suffocatingly so. But they lived, on and on. The earliest groups were so well chosen that they came to be referred to as the "Thirty Immortals." The predicted death rate of one every three years proved far too gloomy. Later groups of thirty, however, were closer to this mean; the fittest had been chosen first.[97]

Geneva, briefly, became something like the financial center of Europe. One-tenth of all the loans floated by the French royal government—and the French government was surviving on loans in the decades before the Revolution—seem to have been taken by Genevans. Although not all were taken on such favorable terms as the life rents, they were still very favorable. Others caught on to the lucrative character of such investments, but by the end of the 1780s fully one-third of the most favorable *rentes*, those on the heads of little girls, were still in the hands of the Genevans. The accumulation of capital from the French state that this implied for Geneva went to support investments and enterprises—political and economic— everywhere in Europe.[98]

The royal government was hostage as its fiscal needs grew ever more pressing. It could not face up to the necessary reforms for effective taxation; so it floated more loans, endowed more Immortals, and continually lost face. But for Geneva and her girls it was Paradise. The collapse, "un catastrophe inconcevable," of course, came in 1789 with the beginning of the Revolution in France. What occurred was a virtual repudiation of such annuities by the revolutionary government in Paris and the rapid erosion of the always rather artificial centrality of Geneva in international finance.[99] We are not told what happened to the girls and women, but since they came from aristocratic and *haut bourgeois* families, were the healthiest people in that very healthy city, and had already made tidy fortunes, it is to be supposed that they lived happily ever after—for a very long time.

The French case was bizarre. Nothing quite like it, to my knowledge, appears to have occurred elsewhere in Europe before the French Revolution. In the Middle Ages, for example, German towns actively recruited female investors, but they did so less rashly than the monarchy of eighteenth-century France. In the Middle Ages, these towns were significantly more independent than their French or English counterparts. They rarely seem to have suffered much from the kind of routine intervention in municipal finances from their suzerain, the emperor, as French and English towns did from theirs. Consequently, they developed flexible municipal fiscal policies of which the municipal bond market was one that was developed to a high degree of sophistication. Despite recurrent crises engendered by poor actuarial knowledge, the kind of catastrophe that marred the later French experience rarely occurred in these towns and never on the French scale; so the practice did not abate.[100]

German towns, like those in northern Europe generally, usually made payouts from municipal funds for annuities to widows, spinsters, and other pensioners, occasionally including churches and hospitals, rather than explicitly as dowries or the like.[101] Publicists, polemicists, and apologists repeatedly spoke of the importance of investing in annuities to the well-being of widows and other miserable persons.[102] The payout on such annuities, of course, was enormous: Frankfurt in 1428, for instance, was expending 30 percent of its total budget on pensions, "effectively interest," based on this type of investment (with rate of return on investment, an issue to which we shall return, of 5 to 10 percent).[103] For Basel in the same year servicing the debt became a major burden, highlighted by the very form of its accounts: "First place in the expenditures in the municipal accounts always went to the payment of interest on outstanding debts."[104]

All sorts and conditions of women with wealth invested in these municipalities. There are instances of nuns who invested their personal fortunes in these early municipal bonds for regular pensions, the resources of the nunneries to which they were attached presumably being insufficient to support them adequately. (Nuns or their representatives in Italy invested in private enterprises or various *monti* similarly.)[105] German husbands also provided insurance policies for their wives in this way.[106]

To avoid some of the problems caused by widows' longevity (as municipalities competed among themselves for women's funds), administrators did employ flexible tariffs. We have seen how this was the case with the Florentine *Monte delle doti*, which had a schedule of payout percentages based on the size of the original investment and the term for the maturity of the share.[107] In a German example, we see a similar caution: in one case a widow was able to secure a return of only 6.7 percent (instead of the usual 10 percent in her town) because she contracted for the annuity payment to be extended to her daughter at her demise and to her son-in-law at her daughter's.[108] Unlike the case for the royal government in France at the close of the Ancien Régime, age always mattered to the fiscal agents of the towns, but then, even at the worst, they were very rarely up against the kind of pressures that would bring the government of the West's most powerful nation down in 1789.

In any discussion of women's role in productive lending, the most difficult problem is assessing the significance of such lending, both for the economy and for the women themselves. One can too readily invoke authorial pronouncements: scholars are fond of saying that the contribution was "substantial," "important," or "considerable." Happily in this instance, a number of scholars, as we saw, have followed up the adjectives with careful statistical breakdowns. In the economy as a whole, wealthy women (and we are only talking about wealthy women) who had free disposition of their movable property seem to have been absolutely essential to the financial functioning of nunneries and the solvency of medieval and early modern city administrations. They also seem to have provided, as an informed guess, as much as 25 percent of the funds for routine maintenance of the productive resources of many agricultural communities. Their productive loans largely went to nunneries, to other corporations, or to men.

Women do not seem to have been risk takers except under very extraordinary circumstances, preferring real estate and annuities to trade. Apart from their crucially important purchase of municipal bonds and some real estate, the evidence has not been forthcoming to show that they played a decisive or major role in urban investment, a few Italian exceptions aside, commensurate with the one they played in rural investment. The peculiar role of the Genevan Immortals in state finance at the highest level is an anomaly, but it is an anomaly that is rigorously tied to a central fact: it would have struck no one as odd that extremely large amounts of money were being invested in governments by women. What would have been regarded as odd was that these women were little girls, not elderly widows, but the French state, too impecunious to care, accepted investments in their name anyway.

As to the repercussions of women's various roles in productive lending on themselves, no numerical precision can be given to words like "substantial," "important," "considerable." Still, there are some impressions worth recording. We must recall once more that we are dealing with rich or relatively rich women. Even so, usually (the special case of the Immortals always excepted), they were very vulnerable; yet by the careful use of the powers granted them by the varied legal systems operating in Europe and equally careful to put together diverse, low-risk portfolios, they were able to provide themselves with a hedge against falling into destitution in their widowhood or old age and becoming dispirited charges on the state or parish. Long term credit sales and mortgages to those needing them also helped large numbers of women create dependable clients for those times when circumstances otherwise might tell against them. Like pawn-broking and small scale moneylending among women far less wealthy, these financial networks were potentially useful social networks. And al-though they contained a great deal of potential for recrimination (the other side of clientage, after all, is dominance and manipulation), the dan-gers for these wealthy women were surely realized less frequently than when domestic distress loans were involved or when pariah groups were prominent in the networks as they so often were in pawnbroking.

The relatively low rates of return on annuities, one of their preferred investments, must have put the financial well-being of many women in jeopardy during periods of high inflation, especially in wartime. This is perhaps why the corrody, with its promise not only of a fixed annuity (4 percent or 5 percent of the original investment in most of the German examples we have discussed) continued to seem attractive to women even when they could get higher rates, say, 10 percent, in the same region from direct investment in municipal bonds, as the Frankfurt evidence shows. The promise of a room, daily food, and a servant, along with the com-munity support offered, especially to an aged corrodary, by residence in a nunnery, in return for a lower rate of return on investment, could mean the difference between survival and the poorhouse. Compiling mixed port-folios of low-risk investments also helped mitigate the twin dangers of inflation and dependence on any one vulnerable source of income.

More work needs to be done on exploring these and similar issues. Yet the conclusion that wealthy women made, yes, a "substantial" financial contribution to the pre-industrial economy and to the fiscal stability (and instability) of pre-industrial governance—one that, on the whole, brought "important" material benefits and "considerable" peace of mind to them—seems reasonable.

Notes

1. Above, pp. 13–14.
2. Veenhof 1972, 103–23.

3. Harris 1989, 155.

4. Rostovtzeff 1941, I, 101; II, 1279.

5. Rostovtzeff 1941, I, 404–6; III, 1418 nn. 202–3.

6. Casson 1984, 27. See also Finley 1983, 73–75, 185–86; Austin and Vidal-Naquet 1977, 148–50, following Finley.

7. Rostovtzeff 1941, II, 959–60, 1290; III, 1565 n. 36.

8. Rostovtzeff 1957, I, 31, 34, 225–26, 317.

9. Finley 1952, 78–79.

10. The passage in question may be consulted in the Loeb series edition/translation, Aristophanes [1972], ll. 839–47; cf. Pauly 1894-, IX, 256.

11. Sidebotham 1986, 83–88.

12. Above, see pp. 14–15.

13. Pirenne 1937, 124.

14. Postan 1927–1928, 234–61.

15. Lopez 1971, 97–108.

16. On risk as a justification for interest, see Lopez 1971, 73–79.

17. See, for example, the use of *bonté* for municipal annuities (interest on investments) documented in Jordan 1981, 304.

18. See Stow 1981, 161–84; McLaughlin 1940, 1–22; McLaughlin 1939, 81–47. More generally, see Gilchrist 1969, 62–82, 104–21.

19. Duggan 1983, 27–28, summarizes the most trustworthy evidence. I wish to thank Professor Duggan for bringing this and several other important articles to my attention.

20. Brown 1984, 405–22; Wales 1984, 351–404.

21. Jones 1989. See also, but cautiously, Tawney 1925, 107–34, 156–69.

22. Jones 1989, 72. See also Clarkson 1971, 148.

23. Cf. Tawney 1925, 115–16.

24. Powell unpub, 5–7; Queller and Madden unpub, text to n. 39 and n. 39; Riemer 1985, 60, 73; Jehel 1975, 204.

25. Noonan 1957, 73–75.

26. On England, Adler 1939, 37–38 (cf. Franklin 1986, n. 41). On northern France, Kohn 1988, 95–97. For information on Provence, Shatzmiller 1990, 33, and Coulet 1978, 96–97. On the Moselle duchy of Bar, Weill 1966, 289.

27. Above, pp. 38–42.

28. Clark 1982/1919.

29. The introduction to the reprinted work cites some unpublished work that calls into question or refines her conclusions on minor points; Clark 1982/1919, xl. Vivien Brodsky has lamented the "undue prominence" Clark assigned "to the atypically independent, unusually wealthy widow in the late-sixteenth-century economy of London"; Brodsky 1986, 142–43.

30. Conyers 1973, 8.

31. Holderness 1984, 435 (cf. Holderness 1976, 105); see also Jones 1989, 72. These conclusions on rural credit are endorsed in Brodsky 1986, 144.

32. Collins 1989, 455–57.

33. Below, see pp. 62–73.

34. Cf. Goitein 1967–1988, I, 256; III, 330.

35. Bashan 1989, 66–68.

36. Several articles by Jennings express his views: Jennings 1978, 225–93; Jennings 1975, 53–114; Jennings 1973, 168–216. But the reader should recall that, as Jennings himself points out, Jewish women did have a more interesting role in consumption lending.

37. See, for example, on thirteenth-century Catalonia, Assis 1988, 90–93.

38. Davies 1988, 101–2.

39. Généstal 1901; Chédeville 1973, 463–68.

40. Berman 1982, 250–66; Day 1980, 125–27.

41. Pirenne 1937, 118–20.

42. Cf. Herlihy 1990, 61, 63; Power 1975, 89. See also Burton 1979, 25.

43. Jarck 1982, 27 no. 22.

44. Vanja 1984, 208–53.

45. Lavrin 1979–1980, 590–92. The work of Lavrin, cited here and in subsequent notes, was brought to my attention by Professor Stuart Schwartz.

46. Lavrin 1985, 1–28.

47. Lavrin 1973, 91–122.

48. Vanja 1984, 208–53.

49. Raban 1982; Henneman 1971, index s.v. "amortissement."

50. Schneider 1975, 111.

51. Vanja 1984, 208–43, but the data base in general is complicated by the possibility that many mortgages might be hidden under the language of sale.

52. McGuire 1982, 197, 213–15, 248.

53. Valois 1908, 366–67, for a particularly moving account.

54. On corrodies, see Rubin 1987, 171–73; Usilton 1980, 222–36; Lewis 1979, 23–38; Beachcroft and Sabin 1938, 52; and most generally, Snape 1926, 139–47. For some typical contracts, see Elvey 1975, nos. 621A, 740, 755A; Ross 1959, no. 307.

55. Moreau 1988, 154.

56. Tillotson 1989, 30.

57. Tillotson 1989, 32.

58. Tillotson 1989, 31, 33.

59. Tillotson 1989, 13.

60. Kist 1929, 18. I owe this reference to Professor Lawrence Duggan.

61. Geiges 1980, 171–72.

62. Duggan 1989, 203–8; Duggan 1983, 26.

63. Vanja 1984, 244–53, listed as "Vergabe auf Lebenszeit."

64. Thiriot 1926, 167–69.

65. Thiriot 1926, 170–72.

66. See, for example, the 3.3 percent rate of return in early sixteenth-century Nuremberg noticed in *Caritas Pirckheimer* 1982, 112; and cf. the 1 percent return on a large 300 pound endowment of an anniversary mass at the convent of the Dominican nuns of Unterlinden (near Colmar) recorded in the obituary book edited in Wittmer 1946, 101.

67. Above, p. 65, and Wagner 1987, 131 no. 116. For another high rate of return, but on an investment for an annual obituary mass, see Wittmer 1946, 101: the mass was to be supported at three (or four) pounds per year from an initial grant of forty pounds at the nunnery of the Dominicans of Unterlinden.

68. Sabean 1990, 341–50.

69. Holderness 1984, 423–42.

70. Swain 1986, 190.

71. Swain 1986, 191.

72. Clarkson 1971, 148.

73. Archer 1984, 15–35; cf. Prior 1990, 201–6. For the regionally complex situation for many lower class women, see Todd 1990, 175–200.

74. Todd 1990, 195–97.

75. Cf. Willan 1980, 78–79.

76. Willan 1980, 79.

77. Above, see pp. xxx.

78. Cf. Ville 1987, 2, based on Jarvis 1969, 416; and Clark 1982/1919, 29–30.

79. Most proto-industrial development appears to have been financed by men. A good general discussion may be found in Tawney 1925, 43–60.

80. Sabean 1990, 47.

81. Above, see pp. xxx.

82. London might be of interest. Again, more work needs to be done, but there is little doubt that big loans were being made by women in late medieval London; see, e.g., Lacey 1985, 52.

83. Powell unpub, 5–7; Jehel 1975, 204.

84. Jehel 1975, 208.

85. Powell unpub, 5–7.

86. Queller and Madden unpub, text to n. 39 and n. 39.

87. Riemer 1985, 60, 73.

88. For a number of Italian instances, see Segre 1986, 370–71, 414, 416, 431–32, nos. 827, 829, 923, 927, 963; Simonsohn 1982–1986, I, no. 476; II, nos. 1643, 2772, 2775.

89. An excellent discussion in English of the *Monte* may be found in Kirshner 1978. The remarks here are drawn from that discussion.

90. Jordan 1981, 303–5; Langlois 1887, 253–56.

91. Collins 1989, 456–57 and n. 48. See also Hoffman, Postel-Vinay, and Rosenthal 1992, 297–303.

92. Collins 1989, 457 n. 49.

93. Cf. Taylor 1962, 959–64.

94. Taylor 1962, 959–64. For this reference and several others that follow on the Genevan Immortals I wish to thank Professor Thomas Luckett. The Genevan Immortals were first brought to my attention by Professor Robert Darnton. I am responsible for any errors in the description of their complex financial activities. See also Velde and Weir 1992, 9, 29–33.

95. Lüthy 1959–1961, II, 478–559, is comprehensive on these events.

96. Lüthy 1959–1961, II, 481. For evidence of marriage, see p. 482 n. 17.

97. Lüthy 1959–1961, II, 478–559, especially p. 539 on the other groups and their fitness.

98. Lüthy 1959–1961, II, 562.

99. Lüthy 1959–1961, II, 559–62; Velde and Weir 1992, 37.

100. Rosen 1987, 373–75.

101. Baum 1985, 24–48.
102. Duggan 1983, 29.
103. Rosen 1987, 373–75.
104. Rosen 1987, 375.
105. Cohen 1985, 246.
106. Rosen 1987, 376, 384–85.
107. Above, see pp. 71–72.
108. Rosen 1987, 376, 384–85.

Part Three

Markets in Sub-Saharan Africa and the Caribbean in the Colonial and Post-Colonial Period

Up to this point we have looked at issues surrounding consumption loans and productive loans in medieval and early modern Europe. Occasionally, the opportunity has arisen to compare the European situation to those in other areas of the world. The value of doing so increases enormously for the period after Europeans began their systematic attempt to bring large parts of the non-European world under their sway. In the beginning, the European encounter was based largely on trade (not least of all the slave trade) and the establishment of trading posts. Except in the Americas and two or three other sites, settlement colonies and direct administration of large territories and populations of indigenous peoples were rare. By the late nineteenth century, this was no longer the case. Europeans began to settle in large numbers and create colonial states all through Africa and Asia. In doing so, they began the process of integrating the economies of these continents more thoroughly into a world economy. European demand helped transform political, social, and economic life all around the globe. The "colonial encounter and its aftermath," as this phase of European hegemony is sometimes termed, had a revolutionary effect on all the colonial peoples, not least on the women, whose economic role is the concern of Part Three of this study.

The precise focus here will be on credit and credit relationships involving traders in traditional marketplaces. Traditional marketplaces have ordinarily been governed by a solemn peace or special laws to facilitate the exchange of goods. The main emphasis will be on sub-Saharan Africa (especially, but not exclusively, West Africa), the Caribbean, and other Third World colonial and post-colonial societies where, it has often been remarked, women have been a central presence as traders in the market, spatially and economically conceived.[1] There is a competent recent general historical overview of traditional markets by Richard Hodges (1988), and there have been a number of specialized studies of marketplaces and marketing in Africa among which an older but impressive collection of articles appeared in 1962 under the editorship of Paul Bohannon and George Dalton.[2] The study of women and economic development in the Third

World has also reached maturity.[3] Curiously, however, general surveys of economic development and frequently even specialized monographs on the role of women in economic development ignore the credit function of women traders and brokers in the marketplace. This is partly because credit, despite its prima facie importance for economic growth in advanced economies, has been undervalued in studies of colonial and postcolonial development where infrastructural improvements insofar as they have taken place at all have usually been government sponsored and financed by taxation.[4] Moreover, as we shall see, women's roles in credit and capital formation were undermined in the same period; so wherever there remained a space in the economy for private traders to contribute to secular growth by providing credit, that space was only lightly occupied by women.[5]

Sub-Saharan Africa

Formal marketplaces did not exist everywhere in pre-colonial sub-Saharan Africa.[6] Yet, according to many scholars, almost wherever they did exist, women played an essential role in them. Or, rather, the leading role of women traders (as first revealed from the earliest colonial records) turns out to have been widely similar over vast regions of sub-Saharan Africa despite gross religious and cultural differences in these societies ("Animist," Christian, and Islamic).[7] In response to this fact, it became widely accepted that the centrality of women in the marketplace is almost certainly pre-Islamic and pre-Christian and therefore immemorial.[8] Throughout the sub-Saharan African regions, social and economic situations in which women have organized, run, policed, and benefited financially from the marketplace (sometimes to the virtual exclusion of men), except with regard to the livestock trade, are repeated. Even with reference to cattle raising and trading, the credit and investment functions of women in the area can be startling.[9] In one form or another, women's leading place in marketplaces has been demonstrated for the societies of the Luo of western Kenya,[10] the mountain peoples of northeastern Tanzania,[11] various ethnic groups in what is now known as Zaire,[12] the Yoruba of Nigeria,[13] the Dioula and other ethnic groups of the Ivory Coast,[14] non-Islamic women of Burkina Faso (formerly called Upper Volta),[15] the Ga and Lobi of Ghana,[16] and various ethnic groups in southern Ghana.[17] The list can go on and on.[18] In the words of one scholar:

"Women are in the foreground of *all* market activities in the genuine old African markets."[19]

Unfortunately, we usually make inferences about traditional arrangements and attitudes from the situations described in the deceptively full colonial documentation of the late nineteenth century; and the interpretation of the colonial record is itself deeply influenced by more recent observations. Kenneth Little raised the possibility long ago that scholars, confronted by the ubiquity of female traders in the twentieth century, were giving more credibility to colonial reports that affirmed the active role of women traders in the centuries before than to those that did not.[20] Nowadays scholars are increasingly pointing to the prominent place of women in African markets as one of many *responses* to the challenges of colonial domination rather than as a tenacious legacy of pre-colonial life. One of the strongest voices is that of Deborah Pellow, who finds no persuasive evidence of female control of the marketplace in pre-colonial Ghana (among the Adabraka).[21] Another voice is that of Keith Hart, who believes that there was very little marketing at all before the colonial era and that which existed (namely, long-distance trade in gold and ivory and trade in slaves) was in the hands of men. Only colonial "urbanization and rural development," with men "tak[ing] up most cash-cropping and wage labour opportunities," provided women with the opportunity to move "into a position of dominance as small- and middle-level traders."[22] Julian Clarke has argued that Yoruba women only moved into trading in the colonial period.[23] On the other side of the continent, in Zambia, women only came to some prominence in marketing in the late and post-colonial period.[24]

Some scholars have suggested, specifically for the Yoruba, that the path to female domination of trade—or, at least, certain kinds of trade—involved a series of steps in which the imposition of colonial regimes was either the most important or the final factor in establishing female control of markets. In one scenario, scholars invoke "tribal" violence before colonial domination as a causative factor opening up a place for women traders. In this view of things, women are said to have enjoyed a special peace in the truces that interrupted warfare. Women, therefore, became the locus of interaction—including economic interaction—among rival factions.[25] As we have seen already in other contexts, war has frequently acted as a solvent of established financial and social arrangements, thrusting women into roles or permitting them to seize roles they might not otherwise occupy in economic life.[26] Isaac Adalemo noticed that in the 1960s in already female-dominated markets in western Nigeria, the civil war encouraged

many female traders to diversify the products they traded in and to extend
the circle of their potential suppliers (with long term results).[27] It is not
therefore prima facie implausible that specific kinds of insecurity on the
eve of colonial domination could have thrust a number of women into
new roles as marketers. Similarly, there is little doubt that markets enjoyed,
as in pre-modern Europe, a special peace in Africa.[28] It is argued, finally,
that the turbulent era of colonial war in the nineteenth century leading to
European occupation briefly advanced rather than retarded the emerging
role of women.[29]

Nonetheless, this explanation, too, has been doubted. A different scenario traces the cause for some recent pre-colonial involvement of women
in the marketplace to a process of "urbanization" in Yorubaland on the eve
of colonial domination. Even if this explanation is true for Yorubaland, it
remains highly doubtful that it can be generalized to the other areas of
sub-Saharan Africa where women have played a leading role in markets.
In any case, according to this scenario, it was an indigenous, but new and
less fettered urban culture, in a social world that otherwise privileged rural
pursuits and the activities of men, which offered women a niche in marketing.[30] In this explanation, too, however, the disruptions accompanying
the imposition of colonial rule (formally established only in 1900) deci-
sively accentuated women's roles in the market as men fought and died.
In the end, women came to dominate the internal marketing system
(including some significant regional networks) and, of course, trade in
consumables.[31]

If either of these scenarios is true, then Europeans were confronting
a system in late nineteenth- and early twentieth-century Yorubaland and
perhaps elsewhere that they themselves had indirectly and unknowingly
created or at least encouraged. Yet as the routine of colonial rule set in,
this system, which they certainly did not recognize as their offspring, was
monstrous to them. European colonial entrepreneurs (exceptional individ-
uals aside) came to Africa with all the ideological baggage surrounding
the social arrangements of economic exchange in Europe, implying that
what Europeans did was more progressive, where it differed from what
Africans did, than the practices of the latter.[32] To European imperialists,
the character of women's roles in the marketplace proved the "primitive"
or inconsequential nature of the African variety (and other colonial vari-
eties) of the institution.[33] Where the power of market women extended
beyond the mere vending of comestibles and administration of the mar-

ketplaces to brokering, elaborate credit functions, vending of manufactured products, and control of extensive regional networks of trade, it
appeared not only primitive but unnatural.[34]

There may have been a time in the dim mists of the Mediterranean
and European past, or at least it is a commonplace among students of the
ancient Near East and the Mediterranean Basin that there was such a time,
when market women ("women engaged in trade") were active in this way,
especially in credit transactions of some sophistication and extent.[35] But
the evidence is embarrassingly thin. Gay Robbins has argued, on the basis
of Theban tomb decorations of the second millennium B.C., that although
such art concentrates on the activities and status of males, it sometimes
reveals the role of women in the spiritual and material economy. One revealing scene to which she refers represents "a woman in charge of a market stall."[36] Even earlier, ca. 2500 B.C., a relief in a tomb chapel depicts a
woman operating in the market as a seller of merchandise.[37] It is doubtful,
however, whether these data are sufficient to sustain the conclusions of
some scholars that women dominated the marketplace or even "partici-
pated equally" in the ancient Mediterranean.[38]

If ever there was a time when such domination of the marketplace by
women or equality of status among male and female traders was the norm,
it was long over by the time European colonizers began the systematic
conquest of Africa and large parts of Asia. To be sure, socially the marketplace into the nineteenth century in Europe was a place of conversation,
storytelling, child's play and childcare; women monotonously appear in
literary sources as central and boisterous characters in these social aspects
of the life of the market. Their ubiquity in the fictional marketplace was
undoubtedly true in practice as well. Yet women played comparatively
little economic or organizational role in traditional European markets except as vendors, purchasers, and resellers (*revendeuses*) of eggs and dairy
products. It has been said that such activity—especially exchange for resale—"activated" markets (the example is early modern France).[39] These
activities often extended to a few other consumables and "female" manufactures like ribbon, but rarely to grain and wine or a wide range of
manufactures or consumer durables. Occasionally *revendeuses* of female
manufactures and dairy products could provide significant income for
families.[40] Moreover, under certain conditions such as persistent under-
employment of males, which increased the significance of the female contribution to household income, the role of women in marketing and the

credit nexus could noticeably increase in Europe. This was the case, for instance, among the female lace makers and traders of Velay in eighteenth-century France studied by Olwen Hufton.[41]

Yet, exceptions notwithstanding, as a group women did not dominate the marketplaces in Europe in terms of the amount of money or of goods or the kinds of goods that passed from or to them. There is little or no evidence that they formally petitioned to have markets licensed. Formal authority was rarely if ever given to women to organize a market or to decide who had access to stalls or booths to sell their products. Nowhere in Europe did women as a matter of course police the market in a formal sense.

Nineteenth-century Europeans, therefore, saw similarities between African markets and their own in the prominent presence of women and the trade in comestibles, but they soon recognized that the similarities belied the awesome contrasts. They also were constrained, at least in the beginning, to recognize that despite the offputting contrasts, temporarily there was very little that could be done except work through existing mechanisms, meaning powerful indigenous market women, to provision their garrisons and engage in most other forms of trade. Traders in commodities that came from really long distances were mostly male, though even they frequently had to sell their products to the women marketers for resale to consumers or buyers in bulk.

Thus, for most Europeans who maintained a presence in Africa—in garrison towns, entrepots, and, increasingly, administrative towns and cities in the nineteenth and early twentieth century—there was at first little or no alternative to dealing with women traders.[42] If Europeans wanted to fulfil their material needs and secure native commodities for trade, even international trade at times, they had to work through women traders. I have already suggested that women traders had real power in the marketplace. To be sure, it may well have been the case that in pre-colonial times the authorization of markets, whether or not they were of the type where female participation was high, lay with male authorities—chiefs, shamans, elders.[43] But important as such formal authorization was, it was the only power that was uniquely exercised by non-traders themselves. The consequences for women were enormous. Market supervisors were frequently women. Their power was so great, as, for example, in Iboland, where marketing was only a part-time activity of women, that they have come to be known in the literature as "queens" of the marketplace. Market law enforcement was likewise often in the hands of women.[44] Forestalling, the shadowy activity on the edge (physically and conceptually) of legitimate marketing, was also very much in the hands of (marginal) women,[45] although disreputable men might be found in this milieu as well.[46]

Such formal power in the hands of women was paralleled by their control of productive resources, especially credit.[47] Before commercialization, credit is discernible only faintly and, with a few exceptions, seems mostly to have been short-term and to have been characterized in part at least by the existence of no-interest loans (delayed repayment at cost).[48] But though individual loan transactions were small and, given their similarity to gift-exchange, of a "primitive" order, these female-organized credit networks, which persisted into colonial and post-colonial times, were "large and complex."[49] Over time, as we shall see, the reach and the sorts of commodities affected by these credit networks changed considerably. The more they affected regional trade, manufactured articles, or materials in bulk for re-export, the more they seemed unnatural to Europeans.

Colonial entrepreneurs and governments in their wake, even while working through these market authorities and plugging into the female-dominated credit nexus, naturally tried to refashion the system.[50] They encountered significant, sometimes successful resistance; rarely was there cooperation.[51] Even when colonial or post-colonial authorities succeeded in displacing formal female control of the market, substantial informal control remained in the hands of women.[52] To some extent, therefore, it was easier to bypass existing marketplaces or to leave them to consumables and consumer durables.[53] Almost from the beginning of our documentary sources, therefore, we begin to find evidence of Europeans privileging those males involved in long-distance trade and dealing directly with them rather than through female intermediaries in the traditional marketplace. In part this development took place in the wake of exploding metropolitan demand and of colonial entrepreneurs' refusal to extend credit to female producers or marketers or to help indigenous female creditors augment their resources so as to lend to indigenous producers to help meet this demand. Janet MacGaffey has uncovered the pattern in colonial Zaire; Kathleen Staudt in western Kenya; and Cheryl Johnson in Nigeria.[54] Indeed, it has been uncovered nearly everywhere.[55] Small groups of men, therefore, benefited. Who were these men? This is a vexing question.

The network of male traders that emerged was far larger than that which had existed in traditional long-distance trade. What seems certain is that the imposition of colonial regimes partly helped undermine traditional sex roles by stimulating or enhancing immigration, since the new administrative units carved out by the colonial powers were only marginally related to traditional "boundaries." Some of this migration brought Syrian, Lebanese, and Indian merchants and merchant capital to Africa.[56] But the most flamboyant example of the mixing of cultures that resulted occurred perhaps in Sierra Leone. There a very complex society emerged from Afro-Nova Scotians, known as Creoles or Krios, who immigrated to Africa, and Afro-Jamaicans (Maroons), who did so as well. Both groups carried with them the residue of various African cultural traits derived from various subcultures to which their ancestors had belonged before being transported to the New World. They also carried with them unique cultural characteristics associated with their lives in Nova Scotia and Jamaica. This potpourri of cultural traits was then (re)introduced into an African context. Notions of female financial "autonomy" or something like it were revived, borrowed, or invented as other Africans were introduced into the colony by the British. There were waves and peaks of female trader activity in this demographic chaos, but there were also significant roles for men, obviously in long-distance trade but also in small- and mid-level commerce. Europeans occasionally extended credit to women, but often at the request of intermediaries, a number of whom were males, undoubtedly immigrants, whom they preferred to deal with.[57]

Of course, Sierra Leone for all its interest was exceptional. Relatively "free" migration occurred, usually within the rather more circumscribed newly established administrative borders (which became the borders of the post-colonial African states). Such migration was stimulated by the desire for distant products in the metropolitan states, the new cities of the colonies, around trading centers, and at garrison points. In these ever more commercialized markets, foreigners (Asians and north Africans) and immigrant African males were central. We have already seen that long-distance trade was already largely in their hands in the immediate pre-colonial period.[58] But male caravaners not infrequently sold their products to female marketers for resale. The Europeans intervened and dealt directly with the men instead. (This occurred in other colonial environments as well.)[59] The profits to be reaped and the relative freedom of migration encouraged more and more men to turn to trade. In some cases, what African men would never be in their home region (stallholders in the marketplace), they would be as "sojourners" in a different ethnic area to which they now had access because of the freedom of travel and commerce associated with districts under colonial administration. As competition among themselves stiffened, these males increasingly began to undermine female regional networks of trade, brokering, access to credit, trade in manufactured goods, even administration of the marketplace. Forestallers and other marginal males began to deal in consumables and to do so in more commercial ways than those characteristic of traditional women marketers.[60] Profits were such that the example of immigrants and marginals helped encourage non-immigrant men to enter the competition as well.[61]

The process of commercialization may have provided short term material benefits to indigenous women marketers. To be sure, pre-colonial marketing relations were based, or so it is assumed, on geniality, neighborliness, and friendship. Money was used, but the markets themselves, dreamy-eyed scholars contend, were not dominated by a commercial ethic.[62] If this idyllic situation ever existed (and it has been disputed),[63] in the first flush of colonial commercialization those women marketers who were "willing" to commercialize their operations exploited this affective network (sometimes to the point of destroying it); as a result they probably benefited financially and in overall access to products for their own and their families' consumption. The same scenario has been suggested for the cities that have undergone more recent rapid demographic expansion; female traders benefited from increased demand until new traders, male and/or female, were recruited into the business.[64] In some regions, the legacy of this early positive enhancement of female roles in trade persisted; or, at least, in one or two regions women have continued to be active even in long-distance trade.[65] However, men have gradually tended to displace women in all the more lucrative aspects of trading.[66] Those women who contrived to stay afloat in this increasingly masculine world were sometimes forced to borrow from men (kinsmen), an act that was, in social contexts where such cross-gender, intra-familial borrowing was traditionally frowned upon, a particularly degrading alternative.[67] Most women traders ever more steadily concentrated their activity on what might be called domestic products.[68]

There were, of course, other social contexts or cultures where the reciprocal relations between men and women were such that borrowing and lending were much less freighted with issues like "degradation" or "debasement." Non-Islamic women of Burkina Faso in traditional households controlled their own wealth, but were not inhibited in borrowing from their husbands (and other kin) to create capital for investment. With this capital, they went into brewing and created vertical ties of production (and, implicitly, credit) with other women. "Large brewers," writes Mahir

Saul, "establish ties with . . . small groups of women who take turns at brewing and selling each other's beer." From these close working relations emerge extremely strong networks of trust and credit (in both the personal and financial sense). Some of the language of trust may mask the cruder manipulative aspects of credit, but the sense of solidarity in this particular instance may not be misleading. Moreover, because the marketing of sorghum beer was marginal to colonial interests (that is, had low profit margins) and continues to be marginal in regional, national, and international trade, it was never transformed under late colonial or post-colonial regimes. At the same time, because economic development in Burkina Faso has been so dismal, brewing remains a major part of the economy.[69]

The "success," as measured by the persistence of female entrepreneurs in Burkina Faso, owes much to the *rural* locus of sorghum beer production, marketing, and consumption. Traditional sex roles were battered by the growth of European-style cities, whose social and economic life was based on metropolitan models. Among the Ga of Ghana the pattern long existed of women's separate control of their own property, a pattern made attractive in part by the loose ties associated with kinds of "marriage" among the Ga that did not conform to European norms. Although, as Robertson has observed, there was a "Ga ethic against lending," the frequent dependency of husbands on their wives' fiscal resources gave their wives leverage over them. They exercised this leverage through making their husbands debtors to them, though at lesser rates of interest than they might charge to other family members or non-kinfolk or even at no interest at all. The system was one of "high-risk." Husbands grew angry at the denial of loans to them; relatives in general were not always in a position to satisfy the women lenders except with services which might provoke in the borrowers a resentful kind of dependency as much as it did gratitude and solidarity. Despite the internal tensions, the system persisted because it was situated within a hegemonic ideology of reciprocity. Husbands had a moral right to credit from their wives, for example, because the children whom they fathered were regarded as their contribution to their wives' support in old age; collaterals might provide other support.[70] The line between lending and charity was blurred.

How did colonialism affect this situation? While Ga-type marriages were recognized by British colonial and post-independence Ghanaian law, European norms came to dominate in urban areas; this gave husbands greater control of resources (as wage earners) while expecting them to support their wives, although they were not necessarily eager or prone to do so. Consequently, women who wished to exercise traditional controls over their husbands in line with the "old system" did not on the whole command the financial resources to do so. Ties based on intra-familial lending continued to be strong, however, and quintessentially traditional solely when the parties were mothers and daughters; no obvious challenge to Ga norms came in this sector from the newer European models of family life.[71]

Colonialism or, rather, the monetization of local economies and the perceived necessity to produce for a large commercial market, had an alarming potential for radically undermining traditional economic solidarities in other ways as well. Margaret Hay does not romanticize the pre- or early colonial environment in which, as a case in point, the Luo women of western Kenya played a significant role in economic production and marketing of grain. Recognizing that "differences in wealth" were a characteristic feature of pre-colonial societies, she argues nonetheless from two related positions that disparities in wealth produced diverse social relationships before and after colonization. Earlier, wealth had been "visible"—a good harvest and a granary filled to the brim to show it; with monetization and "cash profits" dissembling became easier ("I produced a large crop, but the agent only paid me . . ."). Social relationships ceased to be grounded in basic trust. A consequence of this fact, of signal importance in Hay's analysis, is that recurrent subsistence crises (caused or exacerbated by the export of staples) no longer evinced straightforward help from those neighbors and kin who had become tied into the marketing of staples. Or, in Hay's words, whereas it had been "virtually impossible [for women with surpluses] to refuse to give grain" in pre-colonial subsistence crises, it was only "difficult" to hold back monetary credit from poor risks in the colonial era. Women with access to locally large supplies of grain in the colonial period automatically hoarded that grain when there was a natural or commercially induced regional grain shortage. It made no economic sense to give it away or lend it gratis as charity when substantial profits were to be made by working through an agent.[72]

This description of the experiences of Ga and Luo women makes it seem as though they were unanimously committed to the ideals of the past and that circumstances forced them to give up "traditions." Tradition is presented as if it were universally valued: these women wanted to trade and they wanted to trade in what, we are to assume, was the affective, non-commercial way their mothers did before them. However, this may be misleading—and not simply with regard to the sentimental picture of

pre-colonial exchange. Most baldly stated, the presumption that the traditional assignment of women to the economic role of trader was status
enriching—in modern parlance, gave them "autonomy"—may be wrong.
Yes, there were social "rewards" for marketing: the pleasures of gossip,
reinforcement of kinship ties otherwise attenuated by leaving home for
marriage, and so on.[73] But the harvest of a set of social benefits is not the
same as the enrichment of status.

In a society like modern America's, dominated ideologically by middle
class norms, pundits have regarded the emancipation of women from domestic roles as enriching and as being perceived so by women. When an
American woman in the 1970s opened a boutique, common speech labeled
her "liberated," and it was fashionable in many circles to compare her
activity favorably to that of the "traditional" homemaker. But where trading in the marketplace constitutes the restricted locus for female activity
and where such trading is devalued (that is, where it neither bestows political authority nor is attractive to men),[74] women themselves may find
the financial influence associated with trading less enhancing of self-image
than Western observers think it should be and the sex-role stereotyping
aspects of the so-called "traditional culture" that gives them dominance in
the marketplace less worthy of defending.[75] The conventional interpretation of the positive nature of marketing on self-image also ignores the
destination of the profits: for those regions where husbands absorb their
wives' profits, the conventional interpretation seems particularly shaky.[76]

For comparison, we might consider rural Java and parts of Korea
where the "majority of traders and customers" in markets are women
(Java)[77] or where "women are predominant" in the marketplace (Korea).[78]
Scholars have made the same point, namely, that it is "ethnocentric" to
think that the forms of work privileged in the West must be equally privileged elsewhere.[79] Women may be in the marketplace precisely because
they are of low status; they may be kept there to keep them low.[80] It can
still be argued, of course, that the role of trader provides "a much stronger
basis for adjustment to an emancipated status" when that comes.[81] One
might say the same thing, for example, about Hausa women living in strict
Islamic seclusion who, nevertheless, the general economic climate permitting, do considerable trading in their houses (with children serving as runners), organize extensive credit networks, and have skirted the Islamic
ban on usury in creative ways.[82] When and if emancipation comes, these
women, too, may have a solid "basis for adjustment." But that is a very
different argument indeed.

The modernist prejudice described above has been detected even in studies of ancient markets. When Henry Fischer discovered that tomb chapel reliefs of the third millennium B.C. in Egypt depicted women predominantly as purchasers in the market and rarely as sellers, he intimated that this showed a powerlessness among the women of this period in ancient Egypt. When challenged on the point, however, he confessed that status and prestige were socially constructed and did not flow inevitably from control of vending, which in an array of social systems might impart relatively low status to women.[83] So, too, in proto-colonial Africa women who wished to pursue activities besides trade in consumables customarily could find the way blocked for them. Start-up money, as Pellow shows for the Adabraka in Ghana, was given or lent by parents and kin, including husbands, to those women who would set up stalls in the marketplace,[84] not to those who wanted to pursue other activities requiring start-up capital. The extending of gifts and credit, even though the amount of money and/or goods required to start up was small ("low investment requirements"),[85] becomes, in this light, a method to "force" or "coerce" entry into trading. Inevitably, some women, without at all countenancing the brutality of the colonial or post-colonial regimes, could regard the disruption of customary practices in a not entirely negative light and would try to make the best of a bad thing. In any case, the "illusion," as Keith Hart calls it, of believing that African women have authority and status in their societies because of "their greater control of the liquid wealth afforded by trade" needs to be shattered. "Such a perspective," he rightly insists, willfully "ignores the fact that the upper echelons of both colonial and post-colonial society have been unequivocally dominated by men."[86]

Most women do seem to have found the status of trader satisfying or at least not so dissatisfying that they abandoned it, bemoaned it, or thought they had a viable alternative. The numbers alone prove as much: not only have women predominated in the marketing of consumables and consumer durables, but in many regions 70 percent, 85 percent, even 90 percent of all women have been traders or stallholders at any one time.[87] Consequently, on the whole observers and scholars have documented continued resentment among African women to the slippage they suffered in the transformation of economic life under the colonizers. That resentment lasted a long time. Ghana again provides us with an example. While the region marked on a modern map as Ghana may in pre-colonial times have been one where immigrants (or "strangers" in the specialized vocabulary of anthropologists) were regarded less threateningly than in other regions, there is no doubt that there as elsewhere in sub-Saharan Africa colonialism and its legacy disrupted longstanding immigrant-local relationships. The colonial hegemony, as we have seen, augmented migration; at the same time, European-style nationalism profoundly affected both local elites and the masses in the immediate post-colonial world. Nationalist forces put pressure on the immigrant communities in precisely the same way as "statebuilders" in the European Middle Ages identified and harassed minorities that might be construed as "aliens" in a bid to excite support from the majority for its programs of territorial and ideological consolidation. The method used in the Middle Ages was to target those categories of relationships between the allegedly alien minority and the majority that were already loci of disputes, like moneylending, and present the government as a protector of popular interests.[88]

In Ghana a locus of disputes was the market.[89] Immigrant African men who dealt in consumables had long had peripheral places in the markets run by women. Immigrant males obtained this toehold because their contacts with their regions of origin gave them an advantage in gaining access to products not directly available to local women marketers. As long as the immigrant males were few in number, their presence—and, steadily, the growing presence of their wives and children—was tolerated. If that presence had increased rapidly and significantly under pre- or early colonial conditions, local women might have barred them from direct access to the market, treating them instead as middlemannish traders obliged to discharge their goods to local marketers for resale; also, local marketers would have maintained their control over them by the credit arrangements characteristic of middleman-marketer relationships. But in pre- and proto-colonial times, immigrants were a relatively minor presence as stallholders in the marketplace, a presence so minor that they could be tolerated or simply ignored.

However, the immigration that occurred after the colonial administration was in place was more subversive, since it was difficult, given the new power relationships, for local marketers to protect their interests. That is to say, to the extent that the British had a policy toward local markets in Ghana it did not favor female monopolization or control (including the right to exclude aliens). Consequently, the increasingly high percentage of immigrant male participation as stallholders in marketplaces clashed with the local ("nativist") ideology that favored both female authority and a low percentage of male marketers who were, at best, to deal with a very restricted range of products. Once the colonial government was succeeded by the "national" one, it was only a matter of time before the conflict was "corrected."[90] A particularly relevant set of market riots against immigrant stallholders (perceived undoubtedly as British flunkies) took place in 1953, that is, when the gradual withdrawal of British power was becoming a certainty. Focusing as they did on aliens, the acts took on a certain nationalist tint: the post-colonial state enunciated a complementary policy and sixteen years later formally expelled remaining aliens, mostly Nigerians. (The scholarly use of the national label Nigerian, rather than the traditional ethnic or linguistic labels, itself speaks volumes about the colonial transformation.)

Yet it is only fair to add that the scenario described here applied only to male immigrants. The immigrant wives of these traders had also set up in the marketplaces; unlike their husbands who dealt in specialty consumables from their regions of origin, they dealt in the kind of household goods that many local women marketers were trading. Even so, throughout the immediate pre- and early colonial period, so far as is known, the women of the two groups maintained what have been called cordial contacts. Indeed, although rioters violently excluded immigrant *male* Nigerians from the markets on the eve of the post-colonial period, they permitted Nigerian *women* in direct competition with local Ghanaian marketers to continue hawking their wares in peace for nearly a generation, that is, until the state-fostered anti-alien policy went into effect.[91] These women, of course—local and immigrant—did not continue in their networks simply because female networks continued. Female "solidarity" is not an explanation for itself. One possibility that might help explain the phenomenon is that the stereotype of the intrusive alien in Ghana applied principally to males or arose only from "the behavior of men."[92] Seductive as this possibility is, another plausible explanation for the continuity of female immigrant marketing is that it was non-threatening to the overarching traditional authorities as represented by elders and market queens. Those immigrant males trading in exotic consumables had started off peripheral to the main business of the market. Because of the skewing that occurred as the colonial period went on, they began to challenge the hegemonic role of the local female marketer in consumables. But the wives of these immigrant males had no possibility of presenting such a challenge. In any case, there is little or no evidence that what is rather loosely called close contacts and friendship among women—non-aggressive behavior and polite greeting and chatting across ethnic lines—constituted a sufficient bond for the creation of cooperation "to pursue common economic or political advantage."[93]

Elsewhere in sub-Saharan Africa similar scenarios were played out, but they did not recover the past. For in the colonial period it was not only aliens (immigrant Africans, Levantines, and south Asians) but local men who had begun to intrude themselves into market relations; these men, many with "European values," could not be expelled by post-colonial states intent on creating nativist identities. So everywhere local women who had tried their best to adapt to colonial circumstances found it necessary to persist in their adaptations in order to preserve as much as possible of the right-ordered set of relationships, as they regarded them, that commercialization and the ever more prominent place of male marketers threatened to dissolve.[94] What kinds of adaptations were involved?

In Kisangani, one of the three principal cities of Zaire, there can be no doubt that while the coming of colonialism undermined the division of labor between men and women in the indigenous society and hamstrung the latter's role in the marketplace and in providing and obtaining credit, some women who wished to retain traditional powers in economic life used male intermediaries to gain access to credit that they could have obtained directly before. Among the strategies were to "marry" a foreigner or an African male with European connections or to borrow directly from male kin (again, a not always happy form of dependency).[95]

In many other regions of sub-Saharan Africa, collective associations of varying types were formed to provide the institutional infrastructure for credit by and to women in order for them to compete with the newly, if only partly, Westernized men, since banks routinely discriminated against women.[96] The exuberance of some mid-century commentators who thought that women would be able to preserve and enhance their role in commerce by drawing on the almost limitless resources of modern financial institutions now seems farcical.[97] The most famous of the organizations that have attempted to fill the breach in credit opportunities for women are the so-called rotating associations, almost always female dominated, which draw both on older notions of neighborly lending and on newer principles of commercial structuring to provide a kind of mini-credit union for the members. Small numbers of women will periodically contribute a portion of their earnings to a common fund; once in a regular cycle each woman will be able to draw a substantial amount of money from the fund to restock or otherwise improve her business. These rotating associations have had mixed success.[98]

Similar "creative adaptations," sometimes of almost ancient forms of association, to colonial and post-colonial urbanization and commercialization—especially the bewildering array of credit cooperatives and more informal credit networks—can be documented elsewhere, with similar results.[99] Almost always the creative responses of women traders to the challenges of male intrusiveness, commercialization, and incipient industrialization are ridiculed or denounced. The post-colonial government view is neatly summarized by John Howell and Dale Adams: "informal credit markets are . . . working at best inefficiently, and are . . . exploiting small borrowers."[100]

At times, not surprisingly, the victims are blamed for the problem. That is, state authorities will claim that small producers, of whom so many are women, continue to seek loans from moneylenders, the so-called "exploiters" of small borrowers, when cheaper bank credit is available. The small producers may in fact be guilty of avoiding banks, but there are compelling reasons for them to do so. One reason is that the differential rate of interest between banks and moneylenders is less important than it may at first appear, at least when the loans at issue are small and short term.[101] Bankers themselves, indeed, look down on the business of such loans, not only because they seem piddling, but because the formal credit institutions they work for often claim to have insufficient information to properly gauge the reliability of clients, a factor that hardly applies in the world of traditional local moneylending.[102] Loans that are approved by formal institutions have an appalling rate of default (35 percent in one study),[103] although the informal sector too can see staggering default rates under the economic conditions of some post-colonial states—"up to four out of five loans in some cases."[104]

However, the resistance of small entrepreneurs, rural marketers, and especially women traders to turn to banks is partly tied up with a broader issue of social networking. Women in rural areas will admit to preferring to be serviced in their fiscal needs by other local women moneylenders or friends, even when the interest charged is higher than that charged by banks, because it is possible to bring community sentiment to bear on these people to extend repayment schedules when necessary. They see little or no possibility of doing this with banks, where they resent the bureaucratic banking procedures and where failure to pay on time is equivalent to default and will result in forfeiture, foreclosure, or bankruptcy.[105]

Long term and sizable credit needs might lead to different conditions, for traditional relationships between creditors and female marketers engaged in large scale trade were often devoid of the social language of friendship.[106] Yet, where colonial state banks successfully provided long term, sizable credit, they routinely supplied it to men, sometimes prefer-entially to immigrant men; they never wanted to entrust significant sums to women. And even if women did manage to draw on the resources of these colonial banks, the fact *never* had an impact on broader development policies. Never.[107] It may be that "assisting women has been a development concern for more than 15 years" now, but it has not had the expected results: [108] post-colonial banks, private or state run, have not provided any better viable alternative. The personnel of the banks do not respond congenially to potential female borrowers.[109]

The situation, therefore, seems desperate. In many Third World countries where economic planners want dramatically to industrialize and to modernize the financial infrastructure, a very large part of the economy continues to be in the hands of female marketers. Regarded by most traditional planners as obstacles to development, the women, some of whom have singular entrepreneurial skills,[110] are ignored, barely tolerated, or even savaged in development schemes.[111] Their contribution to the economy and economic growth regularly denigrated, "few African women are aware of their importance to everybody's day-to-day upkeep."[112] The words of S. K. T. Williams describing rural development in Nigeria could be applied everywhere:

> Most rural development programmes have been directed at men; few at women. Nor has the participation of women been sought. . . . Up to now, they have not benefited from the facilities offered by [educational] extension services, nor from credit or marketing services. They very seldom have access to formal [t]raining of any sort.[113]

Market women, unwilling simply to disappear but profoundly weakened in their economic clout, generate ever more interesting ways for maintaining something of their role in the economy. These ways help preserve what are customarily regarded as primitive forms of and arrangements for credit; yet the very creativity of their enterprise (unsophisticated as it might appear in a post-industrial milieu) may be a testimony in favor of development specialists redirecting capital to them (a different path to modernization) rather than away from them. But old ways die hard: female access to credit in Third World environments, increasingly viewed as needed for development in societies where a significant sector of the economy continues to be dominated by the small scale activities of female traders, is routinely obstructed.[114] Access to credit may not be sufficient for the effective mobilization of women's productive capacities. After all, there is a staggering edifice of discrimination within which denial of access is embedded. But it is a necessary step.[115] There is some cause for hope: the disgust over such a lost opportunity has moved at last from the scholarly journals to the influential public press.[116]

Fishing Communities: An Exception

The sub-Saharan African (and similar) cases discussed above, which have treated chiefly inland agricultural or urban communities, can constitute a standard against which to set the experiences of other cultures and settings that underwent colonial transformations. The primary and most obvious point about such comparisons is that deviations from this arbitrary standard were large. Fishing communities are a case in point. First, it is alleged that fishing communities have always enjoyed one of the strictest sexual divisions of (manual) labor, and one of the hardest to break. But there was less incentive on the part of colonial authorities to try to break it, since manual labor and ownership of productive resources were almost always in male hands. Authorities who tried to modernize or commercialize inshore fishing, a typically late undertaking in colonial manipulation, did not have to restructure the sexual division of labor. True, marketing of fish under pre-colonial and many colonial societies was often, if not always, a preserve of women.[117] (In pre-modern Europe, where the fishwives of coastal, lake-shore, and riverbank settlements are well known, this was also the case.)[118] But in Hindu settlements at least those where strict purdah (or seclusion of women) obtained, female marketers of fish were usually rare. And in Islamic fishing villages (many African and south Asian fishing villages were Islamic, reflecting the late-comer nature of a religion whose initial impact was on coastal areas), marketing was also prohibited to women. So, here again, commercial interests were not confronted with a perceived barrier to modernization that would have to be overcome by a redistribution of labor inputs. Consequently, one supposes, it should have been relatively simple to transform traditional fishing into commercial fishing under colonial regimes. In fact, this was not the case.

Recent work suggests that the gross generalization about the sexual division of labor and ownership of productive resources may not be a pre-colonial given, in Africa (outside of Islamic areas) or elsewhere, but a very early result of colonial skewing of a more egalitarian distribution of power and tasks. We need not imagine a pre-colonial world completely divorced from the colonial image. It is highly dubious, for example, that very many places would reveal fishing communities like that on the Korean island of Cheju, where women did the specialized fishing, diving for shells, lobster, seaweed, and so on, while men farmed and where credit associations under the impact of modernization were equally segregated—the female divers with their own mutual loan societies, the male farmers with their cooperatives.[119] But if situations like this would have been exceptional at any time and in any region of the world, it remains the case that the strongly male-dominated fishing village of the colonial period in many lands may have been a deformation, under the impact of colonialism, of a much more balanced distribution of labor before.

Emile Vercruijsse, for one, in a study published posthumously in 1984 dealing with West African fishing communities, where women certainly dominated domestic trading, argued that the role of women in the labor of fishing had been denigrated because of the paradigmatic image of the sexually divided fishing village. Marketing itself constrained women to exercise control over the product they vended and necessitated their involvement in the labor of smoking and otherwise processing the catch.[120]

Caroline Ifeka, for another, argues that women's labor, traditionally, was critical in non-Muslim fishing communities in the Maldives and southwestern India, two areas she has studied. Women were involved in "net making, sail repairs, fish salting and drying, and . . . marketing."[121] She identifies a "declining contribution" of women to "artisanal fisheries" in her regions of study and attributes it to what she calls the "deepening regional dependence on external capital" associated with colonialism and post-colonialism:[122] "[I]ncreasing control by outside capitalist interests over inshore fishing, processing, and marketing has reduced most Hindu women to small-time sellers of fish at wayside markets."[123]

Even where a strict sexual division of labor is known to have existed, as in the Sri Lankan (Sinhalese) community of Gahavalla before British rule, where women had no role either in the manual labor involved in fishing or in marketing, credit was probably monopolized by women. Under British rule and after, this continued to be true. In a study published in 1982, Paul Alexander found that "All the village moneylenders" in the fishing community of Gahavalla were still women. He also discovered that the "organisers" of the revolving credit association—that ever recurring type of credit-providing institution identified with colonial societies and their progeny—were all women, "and men could only participate in these through their wives."[124] The type of credit they provided was short term during periods of low catches, rather than long term. Repayment schedules that called for the discharge of debts in three to four months establish this.[125]

One can compare this Sinhalese example to two mainland Indian ones, though fishing plays less key a role here. In the first of these, that of the Maharashtra-Baglan Taluka area of Nasik District (bordering Gujarat) near the western coast of the subcontinent, women do not appear as marketers, but here and there persistent researchers have managed to ferret out unimpeachable data on their role as creditors. That role remains shadowy and is almost certainly greatly inferior to that of men, but it is only weakened, not obliterated, even by constraints as strong as purdah and Islamic conventions on the proper behavior of women.[126]

The second example comes from southeastern India, the village of Kumbapettai studied by Kathleen Gough, and what she termed petty bourgeois women of Brahman caste who lived under a stultifyingly strict regime of dependence and relative isolation, in which "the only proper roles for women were as wives, mothers, and housekeepers for the husband's family." Yet persistence led Gough to new discoveries: Brahman women "who had received money from their fathers," other relatives, informal credit associations ("chit funds"), or, if widowed, could dispose of their late husbands' capital turned out to be active moneylenders. Most interesting, with regard to married women in this role, Gough discovered that

> usually, husbands either did not know or pretended not to know of their [wives'] business ventures. If a Brahman ran short of money, his wife might occasionally lend him some, pretending that she had borrowed it from a neighbor.[127]

Students of the diverse communities of Malay fishermen in the middle of this century discovered large variations in the role of women, with their trading and marketplace activity being important in some communities and rather unimportant (or limited, say, to cooked and cured fish) in others.[128] In those where "freedom of women" was more pronounced in "petty trading," these observers found wives "commonly acting as bankers for their husbands," presumably with funds or credits secured from the wives' families.[129]

> It was also discovered that they were equally important as advisers and often leaders in matters of investment. Quite a number of cases came to our notice where men refrained from selling their boats owing to their wives' opinions,

and, *apparently quite sincerely*, gave this as the reason to the prospective buyers.[130]

The surprise of a humane and well-trained observer like the anthropologist Raymond Firth, as evidenced by the words emphasized in the last quotation, is probably a mild reflection of what colonial observers must have felt at their first encounter with situations like this. Again, the wife's role as conduit for capital infusion from her family may explain this extraordinary level of control. In any case, fishermen's wives frequently kept up strong ties with their families, even if they had married at a distance from the center of their fathers' interests. They would combine visiting their families with informal marketing of smoked fish from their husbands' regions, and would bring back products from their familial homesteads when they returned.[131]

This hidden "control" of credit (though control may be too strong a word) and, frequently if not always, the singular role of women in marketing had a peculiarly inhibiting effect on the colonial transformation of fishing communities. The Ghanaian fishing communities that Vercruijsse examined, like fishing communities in general, were subject to striking and unpredictable fluctuations in catch. Bountiful seasons or even weeks precipitated vast overfishing under the impact of colonial demand. Credit was necessarily precarious. Big traders wanted not only to modernize inshore ("artisanal") fisheries so as to be more intensive, but to transform their equipment so that in times of lean catches they could adapt to relatively deep water fishing. But the fishermen constantly had resort to the hidden nexus of short term familial and neighborly credit in lean times (lean times that lasted longer than in earlier periods because of the overfishing encouraged by colonial entrepreneurs). Moreover, these entrepreneurs ran up against extremely strong prejudices *opposing* the marketing of small catches beyond the homestead or immediate community. Limited catches traditionally went to the women for household or community subsistence.[132] In the Sri Lankan fisheries, where many of the same constraints applied, colonial entrepreneurs finally perceived the weakness of their position and began to cultivate the fishermen as if they were family, "to broaden this financial relationship into a social bond" as a way of breaking the cycle of dependency on credit from kin.[133] But the learning came late, which helps explain why women's financial roles in fishing communities were less transformed under colonialism per se than elsewhere.

The Caribbean

Studies of women, markets, and credit in the colonial societies of the Caribbean (and, to some extent, in Latin America generally) have been concerned with issues similar to those of sub-Saharan Africa. Are the "peculiarities" associated with these markets (their deviation from European norms) representative of pre-colonial (pre-Columbian) patterns of commerce and gender relations? Are they the result of the importation of African slaves and their values? Or did they arise from the special character of colonial life in the New World from the interaction of Amerindian, African, and European modes of thought and life and the structural constraints and encouragements of slavery? Once in place, whatever their origin, did things like markets, credit relations, and the sexual division of labor undergo significant transformations as a result of the commercialization encouraged in the colonial period and the colonial aftermath, yet before full-scale industrialization (where that has occurred)? Finally, what has been the impact for women of the push toward industrialization and urbanization so favored by developmental economists in the middle part of this century? Have women maintained their roles in the labor force, their economic clout, or their access to credit in the mania for economic growth? These are not easy questions to answer. Although the scholarship on them has been impressive in some areas, it is still quite spotty in others; all the "answers" offered here are, therefore, tentative.[134]

That Caribbean markets have struck and in rural areas continue to strike scholarly observers as peculiar is absolutely certain. The fundamental peculiarity is the same as that for sub-Saharan Africa, namely, the unequivocal predominance of women in so many aspects of marketplace activity, sometimes to the almost total exclusion of men from domestic trade, though not from "gossip" and leisure activities. There may be exceptions, but the regularity of examples is remarkable. The pattern has been documented for commercial activities in the markets of Haiti,[135] the Dominican Republic,[136] Martinique,[137] Trinidad,[138] Jamaica,[139] Barbados,[140] and others, such as the isolated Caribbean coastal communities (of Maroon or escaped slave origin) on the South American continent.[141] When we have figures, as we do in the case of Jamaica, they are late (twentieth century) but suggestive: 70 percent to 76 percent of traders in Jamaica were women, though the relative profitability of men's enterprises suggests what should be obvious from what we learned of Africa, namely, that men controlled the long-distance trade of certain items.[142]

To answer the question about the pedigree of the peculiar features of these markets adequately, we would need to know far more than we do know about pre-Columbian economic relations in the Caribbean. Almost nothing seems to have been recovered on this issue that would be of value to our enterprise. For the continent, scholars have shown not only that in pre-colonial (Aztec) Mexico women seem to have been socially "the most frequent participants in the market," but that the marketplaces themselves were becoming central rather than peripheral institutions in the citified valley of Mexico on the eve of the Spanish conquest. Like the process that has been suggested in pre-colonial Yorubaland, "urbanization," following so rapidly on a legacy of war and conquest, might well have widened the niche in Mexico for female economic activity in a world where high status remained with warriors and priests. At least, there is evidence of "men *and women* [my emphasis] serv(ing) as market directors" in this society.[143] And there are enough examples, here and there, of female dominance of or significant presence in markets in Amerindian areas of the continent to-day—such as the traveling marketers (*viajeras*) among the Zapotecs of the Isthmus of Tehuantepec—to lend some credence to the theory.[144] But it should also be pointed out that there are a number of examples of continental Latin American markets that cannot in any way be said to support this theory.[145] Moreover, it would be highly unlikely that these patterns, if the theory were correct, could be extrapolated to the islands, where the level of economic sophistication was low on the eve of the European conquest and where the mortality of the indigenous population was much higher even than that on the continent in the wake of the conquest. Under these conditions, older ways of behavior did not adapt to a new situation—they simply ceased to exist. In Keith Hart's words, "the insular Caribbean is a very special place . . . [I]ndigenous populations and traditions were eliminated."[146]

Consequently, most scholars have not felt compelled to consider the influence of pre-Columbian norms on the operation of Caribbean markets. They prefer to see in these markets the transplanting, almost purely, of West African models to the New World, "leavened" to some extent by European notions (such as formal government chartering).[147] This presumes that the West African pattern is pre-nineteenth century or was in place during the era of the slave trade, a contestable assertion, as we have seen.[148] Mintz, who has vigorously criticized simplistic models of cultural transference on the issue of the West African pedigree of Caribbean markets, is confident only that an array of practices re-enacted or paralleled African ones: "Especially interesting, perhaps," he writes, "is the fact that women carry on most marketing activity today in [in this case] Jamaica, as they did, and do, in much of West Africa."[149]

In the same book from which the sentence just quoted comes, Mintz went on to point out that present-day and recent observations are not quite consistent with earlier testimonies to these markets.

> There is no evidence that women outnumbered men among the slaves trafficking in Jamaican marketplaces in the eighteenth century; during the first part of the nineteenth century, most of the descriptions cite male marketers or whole families at work on the provision grounds.[150]

In 1989 Marietta Morrissey concluded similarly for Caribbean markets in general that it does not appear that women were always in a dominant position with regard to marketing.[151] They may have been somewhat over-represented proportionally. This is because some markets, depending on the nature of the agricultural regime (which differed profoundly from island group to island group), were at a distance from the plots worked by the slaves. Masters in certain areas, like the French Caribbean, appear to have been more reluctant to give passes to male slaves than to female slaves to attend these markets.[152] This, rather than highly dubious West African survivals, would solve the problem of the disproportionate presence of women in some very early markets run by slaves.

In general, then, we are thrown back on an explanation that seems to work well for Africa. Europeans in the act of creating a colonial environment helped to bring about the very system they regarded as uniquely the creation—indeed, the perverse creation—of the peoples whom they dominated. In this instance, specific aspects of slavery were the key variables that transformed whatever cultural traditions Africans brought with them from the Old World. (The most recent authors continue to insist on a West African component; they merely debate its relative significance.)[153] To survive, slaves found it necessary to husband their resources and to acquire additional resources in creative ways.

Both men and women were part of the plantation labor forces; men, women, and children produced (or allegedly stole) the merchandise that they bartered among themselves or exchanged for small amounts of money.[154] Some of the products were marketed to masters for money. It is clear that masters did not relish the vitality of this system among slaves. The abiding suspicion, already hinted at, was that the goods being marketed were stolen, either from them or from other residents of or visitors to the islands.[155] Moreover, the system permitted a form of relatively autonomous commercial relations that was at variance with a pristine view of slavery and of plantation economics (and, to this extent, the very existence of such markets has been classified by some authorities as a kind of "resistance" to the regime on the part of the slaves).[156] Nonetheless, markets run by slaves and catering to the needs of slaves and masters alike persisted in the Caribbean.[157] "For many slaves marketing was the principal means to accumulate cash."[158]

Right from the beginning, however, manumissions were taking place that created a population and ultimately a society of freedmen and women.[159] The manumissions were purchased in part with the money accumulated in trade.[160] On some islands this freed population, frequently mulatto, differentiated itself from the black slave population and for various reasons left marketing to the slaves.[161] Many freedmen and women, however, continued to engage in marketing. The most interesting development in their case was for the freedmen to acquire "land of their own with accumulated profits and become independent peasant cultivators."[162] This development almost certainly stimulated the exit of adult males from family marketing, leaving the arena to women.[163] In an elegant trope to indicate the finally predominant position of women, Mintz creates an imaginary guide to Caribbean marketing: the "market woman friend."[164]

An interesting, but incomplete parallel where men were "pulled out" of marketing, thus opening up a space for women, involves Europeans who went to live in the Crusader states in the Middle Ages. As the demands of manpower for war against the counterattacking Muslims increased, male roles in traditionally male occupations and activities eroded. Markets, unlike in contemporary Europe proper, came to be taken "charge" of by European colonial women[165] and begin to look curiously similar to markets of the sub-Saharan African or Caribbean type of that rather different colonial period.

A comparison less remote in time but from the other side of the world is also instructive. Among the Chimbu in highland New Guinea, where there was an almost subsistence economy and only rudimentary exchange, the introduction of a cash crop, coffee, led to the creation and proliferation of markets. But since men were recruited for coffee production and processing, it was women who started marketing for the new concentrations of people associated with the coffee economy.[166] The end result in this area of New Guinea (as in the Crusader states of almost a millennium before), where men were snatched out of a set of existing economic relations by the direct or indirect forces of "colonialism," was a pervasively feminized marketing system. The system was perhaps less thoroughly feminized than in parts of Africa and arose under different conditions from those that prevailed on that continent; nevertheless the overall similarity to markets in Africa is arresting—and all this in the absence of cultural borrowing. In this context the Caribbean experience achieves a certain familiar quality.

In heterogeneous colonial and post-colonial societies like those of the Caribbean, with persistently large numbers of whites, mulattos, blacks, sometimes Amerindians, mestizos, and recently immigrated Asians, occupational distinctions are typically correlated with "race." An extremely consistent body of research shows in study after study that in the Caribbean islands and coastal continental settlements hierarchies that are based on color and that privilege lightness obtain.[167] What Castillo, Silie, and Hernandez have written of the Dominican Republic is applicable throughout the region:

> L'échelle raciale est la suivante, selon la tradition dominicaine: Blancos, Indios y Negros (Blancs, Indiens et Noirs). La condition économique des individus sert de base à la place qu'on leur octroie dans l'échelle raciale.[168]

The consequence is that more than likely the "market woman friend" created by Mintz is black and her role as trader (or higgler or huckster) devalued.[169]

Although trading has been devalued by upper class whites and other light-skinned people for purely racial reasons, the relative financial independence associated with trading has consistently been esteemed by the women traders; however, this does not mean that even the traders themselves ranked their occupation high on the scale of social prestige.[170] But there was even more to determining the social prestige of trading than racial and economic considerations, at least in those island societies where there have been very large numbers of whites. Many of the original white settlers were themselves poor women: in Barbados, for example, they were of Irish background and "mostly . . . indentured servants and their descendants." Discriminated against by the English as Irish, many of them engaged in huckstering. Slave marketers and, increasingly, the emergence of freedmen and women as marketers introduced an element of economic competition. But the emergence of freedwomen as marketers also, to some degree, fostered cooperation, because they continued to have contacts with slaves and created networks that kept them supplied with their produce. Lower class white women hucksters could enter into easy relations with freedwomen hucksters in a way that they could not, because of sexual taboos, with freedmen or slaves. They did so and secured produce and goods from slaves through the freedwomen. Indications are that these white women hucksters "procured [goods for resale] on credit." In the eyes of the dominant English settlers, this interaction, founded on financial and personal credit, was odious: a network of slaves, freedwomen, and Irish women could hardly strike the English of the time otherwise. Indeed, to the dominant settlers this network appeared little better than a den of thieves.[171]

Although freedwomen traders extended credit to female hucksters and higglers of Irish extraction and indeed engaged in credit sales even to the institutions, like prisons, set up by the colonial authorities,[172] they were rarely able to obtain credit or loans themselves to extend their business enterprises. Edward Cox in a study of the "free coloreds of St. Kitts and Grenada" discovered that the hucksters among the freed population who could "obtain credit relatively easily" from white merchants in sufficient quantities to become shopkeepers or "merchants in their own right" were the few males (at least, his examples are all men)—and not only males, but "mostly light-complexioned." He sees in this "both the color consciousness of society and the ability of [these men's] white forebears to provide them with the necessary contacts and exposure for mercantile activity."[173] This model is not replicated throughout the Caribbean: in Barbados, for example, there is evidence that white merchants were reluctant to extend credit to freedmen who were traders.[174] A fortiori they were unwilling to do so for women. The consequence, which we have seen in other societies, is the persistent inability of female traders, right down to the present, to expand, improve, or modernize their enterprises.

In the restricted economic sphere left to women, credit has been organized similarly and serves similar purposes to credit in female-dominated African and other Third World marketplaces. Start-up capital can come from many sources, but is principally accumulated from friends (prefer-entially) or family.[175] On some islands, like Jamaica, the preference for friends and potential suppliers over family is significant and, we may suspect, might well reflect rather than merely parallel what is true of a few parts of West Africa: the denigration of being financially dependent on kin.[176]

Elsewhere quite the opposite is true. George Simpson in a pioneering study of north Haitian familial institutions in 1942 pointed to the importance of *plaçage*, the practice of men maintaining multiple households or sexual liaisons. Although legal (Catholic) marriage was practiced and preferred (according to the interviewees), the fees were expensive and the legacy of slavery had purportedly encouraged a multiplicity of partners. But the male interviewees never gave priority to sexual gratification as the reason for maintaining several households or sexual partners. "A woman is a valuable aid," it was said, "because she works hard and costs little."[177]

The key factors were cost and return on investment: women in these relationships were advanced capital or provided with the material resources (hut, garden) to enable them to become marketers, to the mutual benefit of the men and women.[178] The relationship, it should be pointed out, was between the man and his multiple partners; it was not among the female partners themselves. The better off among the latter do not seem to have advanced capital to co-wives. Indeed, Simpson categorized their relations as full of "bitter hatreds and conflicts."[179] Curiously, the same dichotomy has been observed among the polygamous Yoruba in West Africa studied by Sudarkasa: husbands frequently provided the start-up capital and expected to be extended credit for their own purchases from their wives in the future, but "no woman ever reported having borrowed money from her co-wife to either replenish her trading capital or to make necessary purchases."[180]

The role of "middlemannish" females and female forestallers and brokers in the credit nexus is striking, if not constant for all Caribbean markets.[181] Goods for resale, as we have observed, are sometimes purchased on credit, the extending of credit being a way to cement business relationships among the marketing women or between producers and marketers.[182] The female trader in fish in the Antilles, for example, buys up the catch from her (male) supplier (or receives the catch on credit), markets it in the local marketplace, perhaps to innkeepers as well as consumers, or hawks it door to door.[183] The increasing demand, however, from tourist hotels and restaurants puts pressure on this traditional network. The tendency now is to bypass the "inefficient" *revendeuse*, whose supply is limited. Hostlers, undoubtedly urged on by state authorities desiring to make

the tourist industry prosperous, turn to so-called *békés*, males with specialized business knowledge who find the possibility of *mass* marketing seductive (otherwise they would not deign to compete with women traders in
comestibles) and who have access to sufficient financial resources virtually
to monopolize commerce with hotels and restaurants.[184] What disappears
is the "quaintness" or local color that tourists in part came to the islands
for in the first place.

Retail credit has always been relatively modest and rare in traditional Caribbean markets: "higglering is essentially a 'cash and carry'
operation."[185] Borrowing of consumables or in order to purchase consumables occurs between neighbors rather than between clients and
marketers, or if between the latter, then outside the marketplace. But new
factors can put pressure on this dichotomy. In the case of Martinique, and
under French influence, the growth of the supermarket is one of these.
The first supermarkets dealt primarily in luxury items imported from
France (a species of long-distance trade monopolized by men).[186] As long
as they did so, there was no incentive for traditional women marketers to
extend credit to their customers. But when the big stores went over to the
mass market and offered a wider selection of goods, including staples, and
frequently at reduced prices owing to economies of scale, superficially
there was no reason for shoppers to choose traditional marketers over
supermarkets. The situation in Jamaica developed in a precisely similar
way to that on Martinique.[187] Given the penury of the general population
in much of the Caribbean, only a transformation in the habitual hesitancy
of market women to provide credit sales to shoppers can stem the loss of
business. Whether such a transformation is possible is moot.

The one alternative to yielding to what appears to be, from all of the
foregoing illustrations, an inevitable constriction of female trading depends on access to productive credit to upgrade existing enterprises: un-
painted, rickety market stalls open to the wind, tropical sun, and rain are
quaint but cannot compete with enclosed facilities. Properly improved
they could, however, be much more attractive to tourists and local residents than supermarkets. But where will the productive loans come from
to effect the transformation? Whereas in the past merchant lenders turned
their backs on female traders, recent history, just as in Africa, shows banks
and development institutions doing the same thing. Women's lack of access to credit from formal institutions is regularly lamented in the recent
literature.[188] The problem is that banks create a Catch-22 situation by mak-

ing so many demands of borrowers. They justify their need for extensive background checks and collateral because of high default rates; some in the Caribbean are estimated as high as 50 percent or more.[189] It is not surprising that the proportion of loans taken out from "banks and other formal institutions" by women traders in one study amounted to only 4 percent of all loans (14 of 349) that they contracted.[190]

The natural tendency is for certain vulnerable groups to constitute their own rather more informal credit associations. Certainly, the Caribbean has a number of these "informal savings schemes" and "partner-type" non-institutional credit arrangements.[191] A recent study showed that 19.6 percent of women in one sample saved money in informal credit associations in Barbados.[192] These associations, however, can mobilize only limited resources.[193] Moreover, they have rarely been valued, fostered, encouraged, or even considered important by development specialists or post-colonial statebuilders.[194] Access to such limited resources is self-reinforcing. Surveys indicate that women traders will come to see such limited credit opportunities as natural or appropriate to their status. This, in turn, will give development specialists the impression that these women, who obviously have classic entrepreneurial skills, are dominated, at the same time, by a non-entrepreneurial ideology.[195]

Consequently, development specialists face the same situation as in West Africa. Higglering, huckstering, and trading in consumables in open markets and on streets look primitive. On the face of it the ideology of the traders seems counterproductive to the risk-taking favored by moderniz-ers. Fostering such activity and such an ideology, at first glance, appears like an invitation for continued backwardness. It is also embarrassing to developmental specialists and political ideologues who share the nation-ality of the traders to be spokes*men* for economies based on such "primi-tive" modes of exchange. In Elsie Le Franc's words many development specialists have "expectations of very little from an allegedly backward and traditionalistic horde of small-scale operators."[196]

In competing with the major commercial and, increasingly, industrial enterprises supported by state authorities, Caribbean women are, there-fore, disadvantaged in the critical need of access to credit. In addition, even in rural areas the kinds of associations that are likely to survive under the pressure of rapid commercialization, being male oriented, big, and highly formal, are equally likely to undermine female higglers, hucksters, and traders.[197] Caribbean feminists, therefore, demand government and private action to insure access to credit for women, including simplification of banking procedures.[198] So far, not much has come of these demands.

For these and the other reasons detailed in this chapter, it is not excessive to apply to the Caribbean what Kathleen Staudt has said about Africa, namely, that the changes brought on by colonialism and postcolonialism in those economic sectors and regions where the imperialist dream was consummated have in general been "detrimental to women" and "distribut[ed] disproportionate resources to men."[199] "In short," writes Laurel Bossen, drawing on evidence concerning markets and credit in modernizing societies as diverse as those of the Caribbean islanders of the late nineteenth and early twentieth centuries, the pastoral Navaho of the 1930s, and highland Guatemalan Indians of the 1960s, "women are excluded from productive roles in the modern sector and phased out of traditional productive roles as part of the process of 'development'."[200] "The social costs of economic development," it has been shown in another context, are terrifying and far too often have a depressingly negative impact on the status of women. Curiously, the authors of the study that concludes on this note were not discussing colonial or post-colonial Africa, Asia, or the Caribbean, but the conditions of life for women in contemporary energy boomtowns in the United States.[201]

Notes

1. Bohannon and Dalton 1962, 55–56, 91–94, 110–13, etc.; Yang 1944, 12; Madrigal 1979, 29–48.
2. I owe this reference to Professor Robert Tignor, whom I would also like to thank for criticizing the arguments and indicating the errors in an early draft of this part. I am, of course, responsible for any errors that remain.
3. Compare, for example, Parpart 1989, a splendid collection of essays on Africa, with comparisons to diverse other societies, like Canada, to the report prepared by the Human Resources Development Division of the UN Economic Commission for Africa (1972) on "Women: The Neglected Human Resource for African Development." (The full citation for the report may be found in the List of References under "United Nations.")
4. Hart 1982, 83–109. Cf. Mintz 1971.
5. Cf. Boserup 1970 and the extensive bibliography of women in development studies of sub-Saharan Africa and Latin America, Saulniers and Rakowski, 1977.
6. Cf. Koponen 1988, 102–3; Fröhlich 1982/1940, 5, and Wood 1974, 10–11, 19, 21–24, for the distribution of pre-colonial markets.
7. "Animist" is a useful, but not very revealing or satisfying catchall term

for the wide variety of non-Christian, non-Islamic religions and cultures of Africa. In some ways, of course, both the terms Christian and Islamic are catchalls for sets of very divergent practices not always characteristic of older Christian and Islamic societies. For example, the charging of interest and active, even public marketing by women, proscribed in many older Islamic societies (cf. the male-dominated markets of north Africa and Arabia), occur frequently in some societies of Islamic sub-Saharan Africa. But the latter are not fixed in their habits; several of them may be moving strongly in the direction of additional proscriptions; cf. the "house" rather than the market trading of the Hausa, p. 96. (It is still debated whether the strict separation of women from public economic life is an essential ideological component of Islam; see Shaw 1981, 239–41, and Antoun 1968, 671–97.)

8. Fröhlich 1982/1940, 30; Handwerker 1980, 12–13; Robertson 1976, 113–33; Wood 1974, 7–9, 13, 24; Arnold 1957, 177–87.

9. Hart 1982, 37: pre-colonial "markets were dominated by women and young men . . . [T]rade in livestock . . . offered an ascending scale of assets [to] . . . ambitious young men." Also Hill 1986, 57; Hill 1970b, 65–66, 139.

10. Staudt 1986, 197–215; Hay 1976, 87–109; Ocharo 1975, 31.

11. Koponen 1988, 103.

12. MacGaffey 1986, 161–77.

13. Johnson 1986, 237–54.

14. Lewis 1976, 135–56.

15. Saul 1981, 746–64.

16. Robertson 1976, 113–33; Hill 1970b, 139 nn. 1, 4.

17. Schwimmer 1979, 685.

18. Koponen 1988, 282; Fröhlich 1982/1940, 30, 33–34.

19. Fröhlich 1982/1940, 30 (my emphasis).

20. Little 1973, 46 n. 32.

21. Pellow 1978, 775.

22. Hart 1989b, 20; Hart 1982, 33–34. For a somewhat different view, see Hill 1986, 57, 141; she believes some long-distance trade was in women's hands "in the forest zone of West Africa."

23. Clarke 1981, 820.

24. Schuster 1982, 110–11.

25. Little 1973, 46 n. 32; Hodder and Ukwu 1969, 24–25, 50. The connection between the offering of tribute by the emissaries (including wives and children) of former enemies at a sanctified place or during a period of special peace and the rise of markets has never been adequately addressed to my knowledge; but the connection seems a real one. Cf. the story told in the *Periplus Maris Erythraei* (mid-first century) in Casson 1989, 91.

26. Above, see pp. 55–56, 73–74.

27. Adalemo 1981, 43.

28. Fröhlich 1982/1940, 48–50; Hodder and Ukwu 1969, 52.

29. Below, n. 31.

30. Sudarkasa 1973, 26, 57.

31. Cf. Sudarkasa 1973, 26.

32. Pellow 1978, 772.

33. Compare the Javanese marketplaces whose dominant women traders were deprecated by mid-seventeenth-century Dutch observers as: "Women who, instead of taking up some honest business by which to earn a living directly, seek to make a little money by sitting all day by the road-side selling a few vegetables and other little things of small value, and do this in such multitudes that they jostle each other and create great disorder in the market place, beside [*sic*] depriving one another of profit and the possibility of obtaining a sufficient living from this trafficking" (quoted in Alexander and Alexander 1991, 372). How could trade really be important, the Dutch mused, if it was in the hands of women? Alexander and Alexander 1991, 373.

34. Below, see p. 90.

35. Harris 1989, 146.

36. Robins 1989, 113.

37. Fischer 1989, 21.

38. Cf. the overhasty generalization of Fröhlich 1982/1940, 32–33.

39. Collins 1989, 459.

40. Collins 1989, 456; Gullickson 1986, 33; Hufton 1975, 14–16 (in the case treated by Hufton, lace, production was female but trading was partly male). The pattern of women dealing in female products may be an old one; cf. Austin and Vidal-Naquet 1977, 178–80, on ancient Greek female marketers of ribbons.

41. Hufton 1975, 14–16.

42. So "travellers related," according to Koponen 1988, 287, in the central Tanzanian case, but exceptions are also noted.

43. Fröhlich 1982/1940, 43–45; Sudarkasa 1973, 57; Hodder and Ukwu 1969, 54.

44. Fröhlich 1982/1940, 46–47; Sudarkasa 1973, 57; Hodder and Ukwu 1969, 174.

45. Hodder and Ukwu 1969, 76. In pre-modern Europe forestallers tended to be socially marginal as well; see above, pp. 27–28.

46. See below, p. 93.

47. There is a useful discussion of credit in Africa in Hill 1986, 83–94. Polemical in tone, it castigates specialists for failing to understand how credit operates in traditional society; yet, with the exception of one or two lines, it is curiously reticent on women and credit.

48. See, for example, Fröhlich 1982/1940, 52–53. See also Bossen 1975, 593; Mintz 1971, 248.

49. Clarke 1981, 820: southwestern Nigeria.

50. The Philippines provide a nice parallel. Apparently there, too, the early colonial period saw widespread trader activities by women only to be followed by "Spanish-engendered constraints" and the application of Roman law, which helped efface but did not destroy the system; Szanton 1982, 132, 144.

51. Adalemo 1981, 71–94: western Nigeria.

52. Sudarkasa 1973, 59–63.

53. Arnold 1957, 177–87: Dahomey (now called Bénin).

54. MacGaffey 1986, 169; Staudt 1986, 205; Johnson 1986, 241; also Bossen 1975, 594.

55. The qualifier "nearly" is necessary because in some environments indigenous peoples maintained their own traditional or modified state administrations even while being reduced to economic colonies. The Ottoman Empire in its declining years, some would argue, was such a case. Though not directly relevant to female traders since they were not active in Ottoman Turkey (Kazgan 1981, 132), the case tells us much. Producers and marketers, of various classes and ethnic groups, who were involved in the commerce of goods to meet European demand managed to turn to a still viable network of indigenous notables with disposable capital for credit and investment. These latter exploited the situation usuriously, but, nonetheless, the endurance of such a system meant that producers and marketers whom colonial entrepreneurs denigrated and, by refusing to extend credit, might bypass in more thoroughly dominated environments managed to prosper here; see Faroqhi 1984, 137.

56. Hart 1970, 107.

57. White 1987, 40–41, 96, and passim; White 1982, 19–33.

58. Koponen 1988, 287–88; Fröhlich 1982/1940, 31, 36.

59. The Dutch, for example, by dealing with Chinese merchants in preference to Javanese women traders in Java established a strong barrier between, on the one hand, all aspects of long-distance trade (handled through the Chinese) and, on the other, trade in consumables (handled by Javanese women); Alexander and Alexander 1991, 370–94.

60. The role of forestallers as a conduit for changes in economic life is well known from Europe, where traditional marketplaces became hidebound with customary rules; entrepreneurs thus bypassed the old system and made newer arrangements during the early modern period of European commercialization and so-called "proto-industrialization" with forestallers, some of whom were members of pariah groups. Cf. Edwards 1988, 124, and Hundert 1987, 259–61, for example on the role of Jewish and Scottish peddlers and forestallers in early modern Poland. Of course, the people who benefited from traditional market arrangements vigorously resisted these new developments or, seeing the handwriting on the wall, tried to adjust to economic change.

61. Cf. Piel 1979, 137.

62. Cf. Fröhlich 1982/1940, 38–40.

63. Cf. Hill 1986, 70–71.

64. Hart 1982, 142; Bossen 1975, 594.

65. Hill 1986, 141.

66. Ladipo 1981, 122, 124.

67. Ladipo 1981, 124: Yorubaland. See also Comhaire-Sylvain 1982, 150, on the evident reluctance of women traders in Lomé, Togo, to borrow from husbands.

68. Sudarkasa 1973, 67. But cf. Hart 1982, 144.

69. Saul 1981, 746–47, 755.

70. Robertson 1976, 124–25.

71. Robertson 1976, 128–29.

72. Hay 1976, 107.

73. Little 1973, 49; Hodder and Ukwu 1969, 51.

74. Hart 1989b, 20–21.

75. Pellow 1978, 770–85.
76. Cf. Koponen 1988, 288.
77. Alexander and Alexander 1991, 372–73; Alexander 1987, 5, 31, 35 n. 20, 36 n. 21, 52–53, 54 n. 5, 61.
78. Madrigal 1979, 38–39. Not all parts of Korea have or had female dominated markets of the type studied by Madrigal; in much of Korean society, marketing was in the hands of men until World War II (Sorensen 1983, 71).
79. Alexander 1987, 30.
80. Cf. Madrigal 1979, 38–40.
81. Hodder and Ukwu 1969, 50.
82. Hill 1972, 223, 268–69, 329–31, 334–35. The phrase, "the economic climate permitting," is meant to underscore the fragility of this system. Participation of Hausa women in the credit networks tends to decline when the general economy declines, even though the desire for credit increases. Similarly, the introduction of compulsory education can undermine the system by taking children out of their role as runners and putting them behind desks during the day. These issues are addressed in Coles 1991, 176, 183, and Schildkrout 1982, 56, 63, 65–73.
83. Fischer 1989, 21, 27; cf. above, p. 89, also for an opposite interpretation of the same reliefs.
84. Pellow 1978, 779.
85. Schwimmer 1979, 688.
86. Hart 1989b, 20–21.
87. Little 1973, 45. See also Hill 1970a, 33.
88. Jordan 1989, 252–59.
89. For the discussion that follows I have drawn heavily from Piel 1979, 123–40.
90. Cf. Hart 1970, 106–7, on the treatment of foreign merchants elsewhere on the continent: "the encouragement of indigenous entrepreneurs to replace and supplement expatriate businessmen (especially Syrians, Lebanese and Indians) has been seen by newly independent governments as crucial to their country's political, as well as economic, development."
91. Piel 1979, 133.
92. Schildkrout 1979, 187 n. 11; Schildkrout's attempt at generalization that all ethnic stereotyping is based on male traits seems highly dubious.
93. Schwimmer 1979, 688–89. The larger issue of female migration to cities cannot be treated here, except to note that there were many difficulties in country women (even of the same ethnic stock as the majority marketers) setting up stalls in metropolitan markets; Obbo 1980, 138–39. It must have been even more difficult where there was "no tradition of large-scale trade by women," as in much of central Africa; MacGaffey 1988, 164 (Zaire). Many such women, in order to build up capital or until they managed to gather a dependable clientele (sometimes never), turned to prostitution. See, for example, MacGaffey 1988, 171–72, on Zaire; White 1988, 146, on colonial Nairobi; Nelson 1979, on post-colonial Nairobi.
94. Hopkins 1973, 70–71.
95. MacGaffey 1986, 169; Ladipo 1981, 124. Little 1980, 109 note, relates a "short satirical description of a female moneylender" in his sociological analysis of the urban woman's image in African literature. As in real life, she used her hus-

band's connections to establish her business, beginning by servicing the needs for cash of the "wives of member's of her husband's staff."

96. One might compare the early credit unions in nineteenth-century rural Quebec, which were set up to obviate the recourse to professional usurers and to bypass bank prejudices against French Canadians; the early credit unions, though not organized by women, saw the membership of women as critical to their enterprise. See Desjardins 1914, especially p. 11.

97. See Mintz's criticisms of Herskovits; Mintz 1974b, 116–18.

98. Ladipo 1981, 124–35, and Sudarkasa 1973, 95, Yorubaland; Miracle et al. 1979–1980, 700–724, pan-Africa; Lewis 1976, 140–41, Ivory Coast; Robertson 1976, 129, Ga of Accra; Geertz 1961–1962, 242, 246–48, 254–59, West Africa; Coles 1991, 176, 183, Hill 1986, 92–93, and Hill 1972, 203, 335, Hausaland; Vincent 1966, 107–8, old Congo; Ceesay-Marenah 1982, 291–95, Gambia. See also Little 1973, 50, 52.

99. Among women: Geertz 1961–1962, 249–53, various regions; Alexander 1987, 83–84, rural Java; Madrigal 1979, 34, 42–43, 74–77, Korea; Wolf 1972, 223, rural Taiwan; Tinker 1990, 38–39, 42, Bangladesh; Stirrat 1989, 102, Sri Lankan fishing villages; Carsten 1989, 132–33, Malaysian fishing communities. More generally, see Johnny 1985, 12, 14–16; Skinner 1964, 20. The relative antiquity of these kinds of associations is established by the existence, from at least 1275, of the *ko*, a Japanese, albeit male-dominated form; Embree 1969/1939, 138 n. 12 (I owe this reference to Professor Sheldon Garon). See also Nguyen 1949, 26.

100. Howell and Adams 1980, 2. For a similar indictment, though this time in an Islamic region of Sierra Leone where female traders are rare, see Johnny 1985, 15–16.

101. Hart 1970, 114. See also above on consumption loans, pp. 25–26.

102. Udry 1990, 251–69; World Bank 1989, 23; Hart 1982, 115–16; Williams 1978, 12, 82; Hart 1970, 113–14.

103. Lewis 1984, 184.

104. Hart 1982, 116.

105. For the case in Africa, see Miracle et al. 1979–1980, 700–24, and World Bank 1989, 24–25. For rural Java, Alexander 1987, 82–83, 151, 159; for Oaxaca in Mexico, Beals 1975, 102; for Korea, Kendall and Peterson 1983, 14; for Vietnam, Nguyen 1949, i, 9–11. More generally, cf. Harriss 1980, 110, 112.

106. Cf. Alexander 1987, 117–18, 120, on Javanese women traders in cloth and their long term credit, sometimes with Chinese men in Java.

107. Muntemba 1982, 93, colonial Zambia. Cf. the situation in late colonial Java, Alexander and Alexander 1991, 380–88.

108. Buvinić and Yudelman 1989, 3.

109. For the situation among marketers in Lomé, Togo, see Cordonnier 1982, 128–29. Maud Muntemba concludes that the removing in 1964 of the legal restrictions on loans to women (a colonial vestige in Zambia) also had little appreciable effect; Muntemba 1982, 93. Compare Louise Fortmann's remarks in a context different from trading. Writing on farming and the activities of the Rural Development Bank of Tanzania, she concludes that "Capital is not readily available to any small farmer, but less so to women"; Fortmann 1982, 193. Kathleen Staudt goes further: "the contrast in access to loans between men and women is quite

striking. . . . Such grave disparities in the initial stages of dispensing loans may grow wider"; Staudt 1982, 216.

110. Ardayfio 1985, 149–52.

111. The literature on women and development is enormous. Three recent contributions to the debate are Charlton 1989; Taplin 1989; and Young 1988. There is a heated indictment of development specialists with regard to their attitude towards women in Hill 1986, 140–45. Her whole book is a polemic of the same intensity about the mistakes of development economics.

112. Himmelstrand 1990, 103. This is what Rayah Feldman means when she talks about the "myth of integrating women in development," as if women are external to a reified development process, when, as so often in Africa, their work is the most productive in the economy; Feldman 1983, 68–69. (Feldman's article appeared in a very tendentious and over-argued collection of articles in a dedicated issue of the *Review of African Political Economy*. By their titles the other articles would be relevant to this study; in substance most are boring propaganda.)

113. Williams 1978, 118.

114. See the two "country studies" prepared by the World Bank: on Kenya, 1989, 23, 27; on Bangladesh, 1990, 113–25. See also Lewis 1984, 173, 183; Robertson 1984, 37; Nwihim 1983, 116; Bangun 1981, 150–52; Williams 1978, 65, 82, 84, 118–19.

115. Everett and Savara 1985, 143–48.

116. *New York Times*, 2 April 1990, p. A17; *Economist*, 10 November 1990, p. 54.

117. See, for instance, some Caribbean and South American examples: De l'Orme 1972, 323 (Martinique); Forman and Riegelhaupt 1970, 195–97 (northeastern Brazil). But cf. Whyte and Whyte 1982, 146–47, where it is shown that in some villages (Malaysia is his illustration) men were the "middlemen in fish, women for cloth and pandanus."

118. Jacobsen 1983, 10–11.

119. Cho 1983, 82–85.

120. Vercruijsse 1984, 57.

121. Ifeka 1989, 107.

122. Ifeka 1989, 89.

123. Ifeka 1989, 107.

124. Alexander 1982, 41. See also Stirrat 1989, 102.

125. Alexander 1982, 59.

126. On credit in the region, Karve and Acharya 1970, 25, 34, 55, 59–61, 66–67; on women's limited but genuine role per se, pp. 50, 56, 63, 74. It should be noted that the researchers were women; it is hard to think how a man could have gathered this information. See also Per-Lee 1984, 190, and cf. Hart 1982, 143.

127. Gough 1981, 251–52.

128. Firth 1966/1946, 81, 224; see also Whyte and Whyte 1982, 22, 146–47; Carsten 1989, 132–33 (with particular reference to credit associations).

129. Firth 1966, 80.

130. Firth 1966, 144; my emphasis.

131. Firth 1966, 336.

132. Vercruijsse 1984, 62.

133. Bavinck 1984, 70, 82–83.

134. I owe a great debt to Professor Joan Dayan, who encouraged me to read extensively on Caribbean, particularly Haitian, markets and provided me with lists of sources.

135. Brown 1991, 158–59; Comhaire-Sylvain and Comhaire-Sylvain 1964, 397–98; Mintz 1960, 20–24, 26–28, 36–37; Herskovits 1975/1937, 82–84.

136. Castillo et al. 1974, 180.

137. Vassoigne 1974, 198; De l'Orme 1972, 322–23.

138. Herskovits and Herskovits 1964/1947, 49.

139. Mintz 1974a, 210.

140. Beckles 1989, 4.

141. On these communities and specifically the women in them, see Pollak-Eltz 1974, 221–46; and Reichel-Dolmatoff 1974, 247–65.

142. Gordon 1989, 71–75.

143. Kurtz 1974, 696–97.

144. Cf. Chiñas 1976, 173. One might compare also Warner 1976, 107–31, and Beals 1975, 148–49, on marketing in Oaxaca, Mexico; Forman and Riegelhaupt 1970, 195–97, on northeastern Brazil; and Gillin 1947, 73–74, on coastal Peru.

145. See, for example, the discussion of Colombia in Ortiz 1967, 393–414.

146. Hart 1989a, 2. See also Lowenthal 1990, 225 (a review of recent literature on the subject): "Crucial to understanding the Caribbean is that here, alone in the New World, European conquest involved not simply the dispossession and reduction of indigenous people but their virtual extirpations. Within a decade of Columbus's first landing this process was well advanced."

147. Le Franc 1989, 99; Comhaire-Sylvain and Comhaire-Sylvain 1964, 397.

148. Above, see pp. 87–88.

149. Mintz 1974a, 210; Mintz 1984, 293.

150. Mintz 1974a, 211 (the same arguments are in Mintz 1974b, 286–305).

151. Morrissey 1989, 164.

152. Bush 1990, 49.

153. Bush 1990, 49; Beckles 1989, 4, 72–73.

154. I was led to consider the extreme case of slave markets by Professor Rebecca Scott; I wish to thank her here.

155. Beckles 1989, 74, 81–82; Handler 1974, 125–26; Goveia 1965, 161.

156. Beckles 1989, 73, 80; Mintz 1978, 333–44.

157. Handler 1974, 125–30; Goveia 1965, 238–39.

158. Morrissey 1989, 53.

159. On the politics of manumission in the Caribbean, see Morrissey 1989, 70–71.

160. Beckles 1989, 84; Morrissey 1989, 73.

161. Cf. Goveia 1965, 227–27.

162. Mintz 1974a, 211, 216–17.

163. Mintz 1974a, 211.

164. Mintz 1978, 338.

165. Powell unpub, 10–11.

166. Brown 1970, 249, 256.

167. Ianni 1984, 38: "In almost all countries, Blacks appear as the second or third race after Whites and Indians."

168. Castillo et al. 1974, 191. The collection of essays from which the quotation is taken is representative in its insistence on the prevalence of negative cultural attitudes towards blacks in Caribbean societies: see Pollak-Eltz 1974, 222; Vassoigne 1974, 205–6.

169. Cf. Massiah 1984, 43; Comhaire-Sylvain 1974, 151–53.

170. Le Franc 1989, 99, 110–11. Cf. Brown 1991, 156–58.

171. Beckles 1989, 81–87.

172. Cox 1984, 67.

173. Cox 1984, 67–68.

174. Handler 1974, 131.

175. Le Franc 1989, 108.

176. Above, see pp. 93, 100.

177. Simpson 1942, 655–74; the quotation is on p. 656.

178. Simpson 1942, 656–57.

179. Simpson 1942, 656. See also Brown 1991, 156–57.

180. Sudarkasa 1973, 118, 149. Co-wives in Yorubaland did, however, borrow from other men's co-wives who lived in the same compounds studied by Sudarkasa.

181. De l'Orme 1972, 323; Mintz 1960, 20–24, 26–29, 36–37, 43. Cf. Chiñas 1976, 173–74, 187–88.

182. Le Franc 1989, 108. Cf. Forman and Riegelhaupt 1970, 198, 209, on Brazilian markets.

183. Vassoigne 1974, 199.

184. Vassoigne 1974, 200.

185. Le Franc 1989, 107. Cf. Forman and Riegelhaupt 1970, on Brazilian markets. In Togo, Rita Cordonnier found some retail credit for steady customers of *revendeuses*; Cordonnier 1982, 129.

186. Vassoigne 1974, 198–99.

187. Norton and Syzmanski 1975, 474–75.

188. See, for example, Safa 1986, 6.

189. Goldsmith and Blustain 1980, 94–99.

190. Le Franc 1989, 108.

191. Clarke 1986, 114; Massiah 1984, 80; Goldsmith and Blustain 1980, 92–94. See also Safa 1990, 81.

192. Clarke 1986, 115.

193. Clarke 1986, 114–15.

194. See Massiah's interesting scheme for reconceptualizing the factors in development, including factoring in "[i]nvolvement in informal savings schemes"; Massiah 1984, 80.

195. See the excellent remarks of Le Franc 1989, 110–23.

196. Le Franc 1989, 100.

197. Cf. Goldsmith and Blustain 1980, 107–8.

198. Massiah 1986, 184, 186, 189.

199. Staudt 1986, 200.

200. Bossen 1975, 593–99.

201. Moen et al. 1981.

Conclusion: Persistent Concerns

As we have discovered in the course of this study, pre-industrial forms and networks of credit usually provided a vital and important place for women. This was true in Europe, to a still uncertain extent in pre-colonial Africa, and profoundly in colonial and post-colonial Africa and the Caribbean. Although the most persistent and successful function that women have served as creditors has been in the market for consumption, especially distress loans (where women-to-women networks were particularly strong), they also had an important role to play in productive lending. We have seen that nunneries largely depended on female gifts and investment, that medieval and early modern European municipalities and national governments attracted enormous funds from women investors, especially widows, who sought safe annuities. We have also seen that real estate was an attractive investment to women who wanted to minimize risks in their "investment portfolios."

In colonial societies the specific parameters of women's involvement in credit were different but just as extensive. They were brokers in regional trade, established clientage relationships with their suppliers, and provided "hidden credit" (both productive and consumption) to husbands and other women even under cultural regimes that severely circumscribed their public activity. Commercialization and urbanization cut deeply into their power. Here we may contrast pre-modern Europe where women rarely seem to have invested heavily in urban enterprises (except government) or risky commercial ventures. The exceptions (in a few Italian towns or in English shipping) are interesting, but the volume of these exceptional women's investments is dwarfed by their investments in traditional rural enterprises and mortgages.

Perhaps this contrast helps explain the strong prejudices Europeans felt for the active role of indigenous women in colonial markets, that is, when the role of the latter exceeded the mere vending of foodstuffs. The almost absolute refusal of European merchants, colonial bankers, and post-colonial development specialists to offer credit to these women effectively reduced them to *domestic* traders in the fullest sense of the word. Again, there are exceptions, but they have been rare and in terms of larger patterns of economic development unimportant. This is unfortunate since, particularly in the case of Africa, the nurturing of female enterprise, many development specialists would now concede, may very well provide a substantial boost to the economy and slow down pauperization.

Traditional forms and patterns of domestic credit—women in a prominent role as givers and receivers; small, short-term loans at high (annualized) interest; face-to-face interaction; flexibility in relation to defaults; pawning; informal credit associations—survive in Third World societies, in immigrant communities in developed countries, and on the fringes of economic life—often inhabited by illegal immigrants and ethnic minorities—in highly industrialized and post-industrial societies.[1] Every sharp economic crisis gives new life to these forms and patterns. Indeed, it is not likely that they will ever entirely disappear.

Contemporary urban Mexican and Chicana women, for example, form credit mutuals in the same way as their counterparts in recently decolonized parts of the world. These credit mutuals have all the neighborliness as well as all the backbiting that might be expected. Carlos Vélez-Ibáñez in a study of such mutuals discovered that "among [the] working-class women in Chula Vista [the locus of his study], *pretenciosas* (pretentious women) are excluded because it is believed that such women will probably not pay their contributions on time." According to Vélez-Ibáñez, the "rationale for this belief is that those who boast of their material belongings are likely to claim that they work for pleasure and not out of necessity. Such claims," he writes, "are deemed to be false and are thought to be a cover hiding economic problems and the lack of resources to meet social and economic obligations."[2]

Class, too, vitiates the solidarity of these mutuals. Women with aspirations to petty bourgeois and bourgeois status, but with inadequate collateral to borrow from banks to transform their aspirations into reality, need the mutuals. But they also crave a certain amount of respectability. That respectability, at least in the minds of some of these women, is endangered when the mutual is opened to illiterate or uneducated rural women or to women of the laboring classes. Those who are excluded feel resentment. Presumably those who are admitted create all the more robust bonds among themselves. Yet even in these closely bonded groups, "unexpected acts . . . occur frequently enough to shatter confidence."[3] The world of informal, face-to-face credit is a conflict-ridden world.

Another example comes from a community of Pakistani immigrants in a British working class neighborhood in Manchester. Pnina Werbner, the author of a study of the community that I am referring to, shows how Pakistani women have reproduced in Manchester a rotating credit association much like those all over South Asia. The purpose, sometimes, is no more than to accumulate capital to purchase gifts for exchange or to provide for emergency expenses on festive or sad occasions. It makes a very moving portrait, since these women, subject to purdah, have little or no public personae. Their world is a small world of husbands, children, female kin, and female friends. All the women seem to be working together to maintain a community under the stresses created by living under the domination of an alien majority.[4] But that very alien majority offers means of social and economic advancement to the men of the community, some of whom benefit more than others. Class distinctions rapidly emerge, and these inform the relations among the women. Tensions among the women must already exist, similar perhaps to those that swirled around the behavior of the so-called *pretenciosas* in the Mexican example; these tensions are exacerbated by new class differences. In fine, Werbner can only conclude that "While women, *qua* women, may share certain predicaments, they rarely form a solidary group" across class lines in the Manchester community.[5]

The persistence of so-called pre-modern credit arrangements and attitudes with regard to domestic credit in immigrant communities and throughout underdeveloped regions should not surprise us. The central issue is not even whether they will disappear, which, as remarked, seems highly unlikely. The central issue is how unimportant, marginal, or peripheral they will become in industrialized and post-industrial societies. It is probably already the case in societies like those of Western Europe that productive credit has lost nearly every vestige of its pre-industrial, pre-modern character. Publicity may make this assertion seem marginally problematic. Women-to-women networks of investment and so-called women's banks or funds with a preferential mission to finance women's businesses are showcased from time to time in the public press, but they do not play a major role in investment.[6] Like the special interest-group arrangements and political lobbying for the aged, for homosexuals, for the physically disabled, or for ethnic and racial minorities, these networks and banks have an important symbolic value. They may, by keeping the problem of discrimination and the unequal distribution of resources in the public eye, serve a useful function in political debate. But their impact on the economy is minuscule.

The market in consumer credit is more complicated. When industrial society was still young, the kinds of credit networks that we associate with pre-modern life were alive and well even in the large cities. In the working class neighborhoods of late nineteenth- and early twentieth-century London, for example, professional pawnbrokers were a varied lot—Jews and Christians, men and women. They dealt almost exclusively in short term loans, as in the Middle Ages.[7] Pledging with a pawnbroker remained virtually a female monopoly.[8] The objects pawned grew in variety slightly as product differentiation occurred, but they were still household objects—watches, bedding, clothes—that is, articles that fell under feminine "control." Ellen Ross insists that wives made claims on those of their husbands' possessions that could be used as pledges.[9] These claims may have been contested by husbands, since there is substantial evidence of elaborate ruses to keep husbands from knowing about the pawning of their prized possessions—the heirloom watch worn on holiday occasions, the best suit, the Sunday-go-to-meeting boots.[10]

As in the Middle Ages, the pawning of domestic objects was the center of controversy and resentment within families and across the boundary of pawnbroker and borrower. Working class husbands who had a middle class view of their family responsibilities or who persisted in atavistic attitudes about the seaminess of dealing with pawnbrokers, could resent being caught in the pawnbroker's web. London pawnbrokers were not highly regarded outside the communities they served, and, the nostalgia of late twentieth-century recollections notwithstanding, they were not paragons within those communities either.[11] They were not likely to have been conceived as Dostoevsky's pawnbrokeress in *Crime and Punishment*, whom one interpreter imagined as "a humpbacked sorceress with quavering claw fingers and a head resting on a chicken's neck."[12] But a husband did not need to envisage the moneylender to whom his wife repaired as the incarnation of corruption to resent the fact that she pawned *his* goods or goods in which he had an emotional investment. It was worse when she did it not for him but for her own pleasure. The topos is the pawning of the gold wedding band and the purchase of a cheap imitation, the profit being spent on drink or the music hall.[13] Wife beating in London became acute, it is said, when a large pawnshop burned to the ground in the late 1860s.[14] Not insured against loss by fire, the women were unable to fudge their pledging: "Where is my watch?" became a disturbing question when a wife could no longer whisper to her teenage daughter to run to the pawnshop and pledge some sheets to redeem her father's timepiece. Recollections of men "knocking [their wives] about" after discovering that the latter pawned their suits find their way into recent interview data with former patrons of early twentieth-century and Depression-era pawnshops.[15]

Whatever husbands' reactions, there is no doubt that pawning was a central aspect of women's activity as household managers in working class London, and they became adept at negotiating good prices for their pledges. "Rings of thieves who invariably employed women to pawn their stolen goods paid homage to this female expertise."[16] Philanthropic ladies, sharing ideas about pawnbroking that a medieval theologian could have endorsed with fervor, dropped in on working class families to determine whether they were sufficiently poor to deserve charity. Pawn tickets were placed in front of them to show the depth of the borrowers' poverty—and to elicit sympathy in that they suffered under manifest usury. Yet, since the pawn tickets served as a substitute currency among women in this world, the possession of an abundance of them, though it may have fooled a few middle class matrons, was no sure sign of abject poverty; indeed, it might well be the reverse. A poor woman who had pawned her husband's watch might need help—food or money—from her female neighbor who was better off; she could give the neighbor the pawn ticket as payment (to do with as she saw fit) or as a pledge, redeemable within a certain time. "Lent, stolen, or honestly gotten pledge tickets were transferred and traded," Ross writes, "in complex patterns between groups of women, court cases show."[17]

That "court cases" show this use of pawn tickets indicates the problematic nature of the trade. A woman who gave her pawn tickets to another woman in return for food might very well give them without condition in the necessity of the moment, but expect at least to have first right of repurchase if her creditor wanted to redeem or dispose of the tickets. In a world of much want the "market value" of pawn tickets, though low relative to the prices of goods and services in markets that served the middle classes and labor aristocracy, was sufficiently high to invite theft. Ross marshals evidence of police court complaints of "lost" and stolen pawn tickets; of stolen goods, pawned, the pawn tickets then being sold by the thieves for additional profit; and of the jail terms that sometimes ensued for the convicted thieves.[18]

On the one hand, where poverty is crushing and people have insufficient income to buy food and other necessities, this model of a pre-modern world of credit will survive. The specific parameters may change slightly, depending on legislation about and regulation of small loan businesses and pawnshops. On the other hand, the level of informal credit immediately above what might be called this subsistence or domestic level has been obliterated—or nearly so—in recent history by the charge plate and credit card. The outlay of money for a wedding gift, birthday present, or, in some cases, food and drink, which would have sent women (and men) to the moneylender before or forced them to save is now available from credit purchases regulated through powerful financial institutions. The strangeness of this kind of credit to a student of pre-modern societies is worth mentioning: the interest rates are certainly smaller than those charged by moneylenders and pawnbrokers in the past. But the difference is that in the past, consumption loans were repaid with great rapidity. The 17 to 22 percent rates charged on consumer credit cards in the contemporary United States cover the repayment of loans over so long a time that the real payback rate far exceeds that for consumption loans in the pre-modern period.[19]

To be sure, not everyone has access to the kind of consumer credit represented by the charge plate or credit card.[20] Discrimination obviously (and defensibly) exists on the basis of age and income and more invidiously on the basis of race and marital status. Women, it is sometimes said, suffer discrimination here as elsewhere in the society and economy. Arguably (though it is not an argument that can be addressed here), that discrimination might be mitigated by legislation and careful regulation. What seems abundantly clear, despite all the caveats, is that the creation of this new type of consumer credit has severely undermined old-fashioned face-to-face credit, reducing its sphere to the world of the most destitute. We are left, therefore, with a deep chasm that separates the poor who have no access to the newer forms of credit and the less poor and well-off who do, with all that that implies for the distinctions of status as calibrated to the possession of consumer goods in modern societies. The anger and resentments, on the one side, and, perhaps, the disdain, on the other, resulting from perceptions across the chasm will be no less fractious in their impact on social relations than the tensions endemic to credit and its denial in time past. That so many women—married Caribbean women with emigrant husbands in the United States, single mothers abandoned by the fathers of their children in our inner cities, war widows in the seemingly incessant chaos of Africa—that, to repeat, so many women are on the impoverished side of the chasm is cause for compassion and concern, both for them and for their children.[21] The disturbing and complicated story of women and credit goes on.

Notes

1. Lelart 1978, 67–73; Von der Mehden 1968, 36, 62; and below, pp. 129–31.
2. Vélez-Ibañez 1983, 91.
3. Vélez-Ibañez 1983, 92–93.
4. Werbner 1988, 181–83, 188, 190.
5. Werbner 1988, 179.
6. Gorman 1990, 42; Nichols 1989, 142; *Business Week* 1985, 67.
7. Tebbutt 1983, 9.
8. Tebbutt 1983, 13, 31, 51–55, 121–23, 131; Hudson 1982, 77–78, 80, 84, 103.
9. Ross unpub., 44. I wish to thank Professor Ross for letting me read and cite portions of her unpublished study.
10. Ross unpub., 45.
11. Cf. Tebbutt 1983, 4, 26, 28, 46, who argues that the image had improved from pre-modern times.
12. Seduro 1977, 374–79. See further on representations of this character, Lary 1986, 103.
13. Ross unpub., 45.
14. Ross unpub., 46.
15. Hudson 1982, 78.
16. Ross unpub., 43.
17. Ross unpub., 43.
18. Ross unpub., 43.
19. The literature on the credit card revolution is enormous. Two serviceable studies are Krumme 1987 and Mandell and Murphy 1976.
20. For an "empirical" analysis of access to credit cards and credit card use, see McAlister 1975.
21. Safa 1986, 9; Garfinkel and McLanahan 1986, 45–85.

References

Adalemo, Isaac. 1981. *Marketplaces in a Developing Country: The Case of Western Nigeria*. Ann Arbor, Mich.: Department of Geography, University of Michigan.

Adelman, Howard. 1991. "Rabbis and Reality: Public Activities of Jewish Women in Italy During the Renaissance and Catholic Restoration," *Jewish History*, 5: 27–40.

Adler, Michael. 1939. *The Jews of Medieval England*. London: E. Goldston.

Alexander, Jennifer. 1987. *Trade, Traders and Trading in Rural Java*. Singapore and New York: Oxford University Press.

Alexander, Paul. 1982. *Sri Lankan Fishermen: Rural Capitalism and Peasant Society*. Canberra: Australian National University Press.

Alexander, Paul, and Jennifer Alexander. 1991. "Protecting Peasants from Capitalism: The Subordination of Javanese Traders by the Colonial State," *Comparative Studies in Society and History*, 33: 370–94.

Antoun, Richard. 1968. "On the Modesty of Women in Arab Muslim Villages: A Study in the Accommodation of Traditions," *American Anthropologist*, 70: 671–97.

Archer, Rowena. 1984. "Rich Old Ladies: The Problem of Late Medieval Dowagers," in *Property and Politics: Essays in Later Medieval English History*, ed. T. Pollard. Gloucester and New York: St. Martin's Press. Pp. 15–35.

Ardayfio, Elizabeth. 1985. "Women and Urban Marketing in Ghana," in *Women Creating Wealth: Transforming Economic Development*, ed. R. Gallin and A. Spring. Washington, D.C.: Association for Women in Development. Pp. 149–52.

Aristophanes. [1972]. *Thesmophoriazusae*. Loeb Classical Library Series: *Aristophanes*, III. Cambridge, Mass., and London: Harvard University Press.

Arnold, Rosemary. 1957. "Separation of Trade and Market: Great Market of Whydah," in *Trade and Market in the Early Empires: Economies in History and Theory*, ed. K. Polanyi et al. Glencoe, Ill.: Free Press. Pp. 177–87.

Ashton, Robert. 1960. "Usury and High Finance in the Age of Shakespeare and Jonson," *Renaissance and Modern Studies*, 4: 14–43.

Assis, Yom Tov. 1988. *The Jews of Santa Coloma de Queralt: An Economic and Demographic Study of a Community at the End of the Thirteenth Century*. Jerusalem: Magnes Press (Hebrew University).

Austin, M., and P. Vidal-Naquet. 1977. *Economic and Social History of Ancient Greece: An Introduction*. Berkeley: University of California Press.

Baldwin, John W. 1970. *Masters, Princes, and Merchants: The Social Views of Peter the Chanter and His Circle.* 2 vols. Princeton, N.J.: Princeton University Press.

Bangun, Masliana. 1981. "The Advantages of Functional Education and Credit Facilities for Javanese Rural Women," in *The Endless Day: Some Case Material on Asian Rural Women,* ed. T. Scarlett Epstein and Rosemary A. Watts. Oxford and elsewhere: Pergamon Press. Pp. 128–54.

Barth, Fredrik. 1988. *Human Resources: Social and Cultural Features of the Jebel Marra Project Area.* Bergen: Department of Social Anthropology, University of Bergen.

Bashan, Eliezer. 1989. "Jewish Moneylending in Constantinople and Smyrna During the 17th–18th Centuries as Reflected in the British Levant Company's Archives," in *The Mediterranean and the Jews: Banking, Finance and International Trade (XVI–XVIII Centuries),* ed. Ariel Toaff and Simon Schwarzfuchs. Ramat-Gan: Bar-Ilan University Press. Pp. 57–73.

Baskin, Judith. 1991. "Some Parallels in the Education of Medieval Jewish and Christian Women," *Jewish History,* 5: 41–51.

Baum, Hans-Peter. 1985. "Annuities in Late Medieval Hanse Towns," *Business History Review,* 59: 24–48.

Bautier, Robert-Henri. 1981. "'Clercs mécaniques' et 'clercs marchands' dans la France du XIIIe siècle," *Académie des Inscriptions et Belles-Lettres: Comptes-Rendus.* Pp. 209–42.

Bavinck, Maarten. 1984. *Small Fry: The Economy of Petty Fishermen in Northern Sri Lanka.* Amsterdam: Free University Press.

Beachcroft, G., and A. Sabin. 1938. *Two Compotus Rolls of Saint Augustine's Abbey, Bristol.* Bristol: Bristol Record Society.

Beals, Ralph. 1975. *The Peasant Marketing System of Oaxaca, Mexico.* Berkeley. University of California Press.

Beckles, Hilary. 1989. *Natural Rebels: A Social History of Enslaved Black Women in Barbados.* London: Zed Press.

Berman, Constance. 1982. "Land Acquisition and the Use of the Mortgage Contract by the Cistercians of Berdoues," *Speculum,* 57: 250–66.

Biget, Jean-Louis. 1970. "Aspects du crédit dans l'Albigeois à la fin du XIIIe siècle," *Fédération des sociétés académiques et savantes de Languedoc, Pyrénées, Gascogne: Actes du XXVIe Congrès.* Pp. 1–50.

Bohannon, Paul, and George Dalton, eds. 1962. *Markets in Africa.* Evanston, Ill.: Northwestern University Press.

Bonazzoli, Viviana. 1987. "Ebrei italiani, portoghesi, levantini sulla piazza commerciale di Ancona intorno alla metà del Cinquecento," in *Gli Ebrei e Venezia: secoli XIV–XVIII,* ed. Gaetano Cozzi. Milan: Edizioni Comunità. Pp. 727–70.

Bonetti, Carlo. 1982/1917. *Gli Ebrei a Cremona, 1278–1630.* Cremona. Tipografica "Buona Stampa." Reprint Bologna: A Forni.

Boserup, Ester. 1970. *Woman's Role in Economic Development.* London: Allen and Unwin.

Bossen, Laurel. 1975. "Women in Modernizing Societies," *American Ethnologist,* 2: 587–601.

Bowers, Richard. 1983. "From Rolls to Riches: King's Clerks and Moneylending in Thirteenth-Century England," *Speculum*, 58: 60–71.

Braunstein, Philippe. 1987. "Le Prêt sur gage à Padoue et dans le Padouan au milieu du XVe siècle," in *Gli Ebrei e Venezia: secoli XIV–XVIII*, ed. Gaetano Cozzi. Milan: Edizioni Comunità. Pp. 651–69.

Britnell, R. H. 1986. *Growth and Decline in Colchester, 1300–1525*. Cambridge: Cambridge University Press.

Brodsky, Vivien. 1986. "Widows in Late Elizabethan London: Remarriage, Economic Opportunity and Family Orientations," in *The World We Have Gained: Histories of Population and Social Structure*, ed. Lloyd Bonfield et al. Oxford: Basil Blackwell. Pp. 122–54.

Brown, Karen. 1991. *Mama Lola: A Vodou Priestess in Brooklyn*. Berkeley: University of California Press.

Brown, Keith. 1989. "Noble Indebtedness in Scotland between the Reformation and the Revolution," *Bulletin of the Institute of Historical Research*, 62: 260–75.

Brown, Paula. 1970. "*Minge-Money*: Economic Change in the New Guinea Highlands," *Southwestern Journal of Anthropology*, 26: 242–60.

Brown, W. Newman. 1984. "The Receipt of Poor Relief and Family Situation: Aldenham, Hertfordshire 1630–90," in *Land, Kinship and Life-Cycle*, ed. Richard M. Smith. Cambridge: Cambridge University Press. Pp. 405–22.

Buck, Mark. 1983. *Politics, Finance and the Church in the Reign of Edward II: Walter Stapledon, Treasurer of England*. Cambridge: Cambridge University Press.

Burton, Janet. 1979. *The Yorkshire Nunneries in the Twelfth and Thirteenth Centuries*. Borthwick Papers, No. 56.

Bush, Barbara. 1990. *Slave Women in Caribbean Society: 1650–1838*. Kingston and elsewhere: Heinemann Caribbean; Bloomington: Indiana University Press.

Business Week. 1985. Editorial Comment. 16 September. P. 67.

Buvinić, Mayra, and Sally Yudelman. 1989. *Women, Poverty and Progress in the Third World*. New York: Foreign Policy Association.

Caritas Pirckheimer. 1982. *Caritas Pirckheimer 1467–1532. Eine Ausstellung der katholischen Stadtkirche Nürnberg*. Munich: Prestel-Verlag.

Carpenter, David. 1980. "Was There a Crisis of the Knightly Class in the Thirteenth Century? The Oxfordshire Evidence," *English Historical Review*, 95: 721–52.

Carsten, Janet. 1989. "Cooking Money: Gender and the Symbolic Transformation of Means of Exchange in a Malay Fishing Community," in *Money and the Morality of Exchange*, ed. J. Parry and M. Bloch. Cambridge: Cambridge University Press. Pp. 94–116.

Cassard, J.-C. 1984. "Les Premiers immigrés," *Médiévales*, No. 6: 85–94.

Casson, Lionel. 1984. *Ancient Trade and Society*. Detroit: Wayne State University Press.

———. 1989. *The* Periplus Maris Erythraei: *Text with Introduction, Translation, and Commentary*. Princeton, N.J.: Princeton University Press.

Cassuto, Umberto. 1918. *Gli Ebrei a Firenze nell'età del Rinascimento*. Florence: Galletti e Cocci.

Castellani, Christian. 1972. "Le Rôle économique de la communauté juive de Carpentras au début du XVe siècle," *Annales: ESC*, 27: 583–611.

Castillo, Luciano, et al. 1974. "Réflexions sur la femme noire en République Dominicaine," in *La Femme de couleur en Amérique latine*, ed. Roger Bastide. Paris: Éditions Anthropos. Pp. 171–91.

Ceesay-Marenah, Coumba. 1982. "Women's Cooperative Thrift and Credit Societies: An Element of Women's Programs in the Gambia," in *Women and Work in Africa*, ed. Edna G. Bay. Boulder, Colo.: Westview Press Pp. 289–95.

Charlton, Sue Ellen M., Jana Everett, and Kathleen Staudt, eds. 1989. *Women, the State, and Development*. Albany: State University of New York Press.

Chédeville, André. 1973. *Chartres et ses campagnes XIe–XIIIe s.*. Paris: Klincksieck.

Chiñas, Beverly. 1976. "Zapotec *Viajeras*," in *Markets in Oaxaca*, ed. S. Cook and M. Diskin. Austin, Tex., and London: University of Texas Press. Pp. 169–88.

Chiuppani, Giovanni. 1977/1907. *Gli Ebrei a Bassano*. Bassano: Pozzato. Reprint Bologna: A. Forni.

Cho, Haejong. 1983. "The Autonomous Women: Divers in Cheju Island," in *Korean Women: View from the Inner Room*, ed. Laurel Kendall and Mark Peterson. New Haven, Conn.: East Rock Press. Pp. 81–95.

Chomel, Vital. 1951–1952. "Communautés rurales et 'casanes' lombardes en Dauphiné (1346): Contribution au problème de l'endettement dans les sociétés paysannes du sud-est de la France au bas moyen âge," *Bulletin philologique et historique*. Pp. 225–47.

Ciscato, Antonio. 1967/1901. *Gli Ebrei in Padova (1300–1800)*. Padua: Società Cooperativa Tipografica. Reprint Bologna: A. Forti.

Clark, Alice. 1982/1919. *Working Life of Women in the Seventeenth Century*. London: Routledge and Kegan Paul.

Clark, Elaine. 1981. "Debt Litigation in a Late Medieval English Vill," in *Pathways to Medieval Peasants*, ed. J. Raftis. Toronto: Pontifical Institute of Mediaeval Studies. Pp. 247–79.

Clarke, Julian. 1981. "Households and the Political Economy of Small-Scale Cash Crop Production in South-Western Nigeria," *Africa: Journal of the International African Institute*, 51: 807–23.

Clarke, Roberta. 1986. "Women's Organisations, Women's Interests," *Social and Economic Studies*, 35: 107–55.

Clarkson, Leslie. 1971. *The Pre-Industrial Economy in England, 1500–1750*. London: Batsford.

Cochard, Théophile. 1976/1895. *La Juiverie d'Orléans*. Orléans. H. Herluison. Reprint Marseille: Laffitte.

Cohen, Esther. 1980. "Patterns of Crime in Fourteenth-Century Paris," *French Historical Studies*, 11: 307–27.

Cohen, Sherill. 1985. "The Convertite and the Malmaritate: Women's Institutions, Prostitution, and the Family in Counter-Reformation Florence." Unpublished Ph. D. dissertation, Princeton University.

Colafemmina, Cesare. 1989. "The Commercial and Banking Activities of the Jews of Bari during the Spanish Vice-Regency," in *The Mediterranean and the Jews: Banking, Finance and International Trade (XVI–XVIII Centuries)*, ed.

Ariel Toaff and Simon Schwarzfuchs. Ramat-Gan: Bar-Ilan University Press. Pp. 105–21.

Coles, Catherine. 1991. "Hausa Women's Work in a Declining Urban Economy: Kaduna, Nigeria, 1980–1985," in *Hausa Women in the Twentieth Century,* ed. Catherine Coles and Beverly Mack. Madison: University of Wisconsin Press. Pp. 163–91.

Collins, James. 1989. "The Economic Role of Women in Seventeenth-Century France," *French Historical Studies,* 16: 436–70.

Comhaire-Sylvain, Suzanne. 1974. "La Paysanne de la région de Kenscoff (Haïti)," in *La Femme de couleur en Amérique latine,* ed. Roger Bastide. Paris: Éditions Anthropos. Pp. 149–70.

———. 1982. *Femmes de Lomé.* Bandundu: Ceeba.

Comhaire-Sylvain, Suzanne, and J. Comhaire-Sylvain. 1964. "A Statistical Note on the Kenscoff Market System, Haiti," *Social and Economic Studies,* 13: 397–404.

Conyers, Angela, ed. 1973. *The Wiltshire Extents for Debts: Edward I–Elizabeth I.* Devizes: Wiltshire Record Society.

Cordonnier, Rita. 1982. *Femmes africaines et commerce: Les Revendeuses de tissu de la ville de Lomé (Togo).* Paris: Éditions l'Harmattan.

Coulet, Noël. 1978. "Autour d'un quinzain des métiers de la communauté juive d'Aix en 1437," in *Actes de la Table Ronde du G. I. S. méditerranée,* Abbaye de Senanque.

Cox, Edward. 1984. *Free Coloreds in the Slave Societies of St. Kitts and Grenada, 1763–1833.* Knoxville: University of Tennessee Press.

Crémieux, Adolphe. 1903. "Les Juifs de Marseille au moyen-âge," *Revue des études juives,* 46: 1–47, 246–68.

Crummey, Robert. 1970. *The Old Believers and the World of Antichrist: The Vyg Community and the Russian State, 1694–1855.* Madison: University of Wisconsin Press.

D'Arms, John H. 1981. *Commerce and Social Standing in Ancient Rome.* Cambridge, Mass.: Harvard University Press.

Davies, Wendy. 1988. *Small Worlds: The Village Community in Early Medieval Brittany.* Berkeley and Los Angeles: University of California Press.

Davis, Myer. 1888. *Shetaroth: Hebrew Deeds of English Jews Before 1290.* London: Office of the "Jewish Chronicle."

Day, Gerald. 1980. "The Lay Attitude Toward Savigny in the Ages of Philip Augustus," *Analecta Cisterciensia,* 30: 103–28.

Delisle, Léopold. 1969/1851. *Études sur la condition de la classe agricole et l'état de l'agriculture en Normandie.* Evreux: Hérissey. Reprint New York: B. Franklin.

De l'Orme, Jean-Claude. 1972. "Les Transformations économiques et sociales d'un marché martiniquais," in *L'Archipel inachevé: Culture et société aux Antilles françaises,* ed. Jean Benoist. Montreal: Presses de l'Université de Montréal. Pp. 321–34.

De Roover, Raymond. 1948. *Money, Banking and Credit in Mediaeval Bruges: Italian Merchant-Bankers, Lombards, and Money-Changers.* Cambridge, Mass.: Medieval Academy of America.

Desjardins, Alphonse. 1914. *The Cooperative People's Bank*. New York: Russell Sage Foundation.

Dillard, Heath. 1984. *Daughters of the Reconquest: Women in Castilian Town Society, 1100–1300*. Cambridge: Cambridge University Press.

Dobson, R. B. 1974. *The Jews of Medieval York and the Massacre of March 1190*. Borthwick Papers, No. 45.

Duby, Georges, and Armand Wallon, eds. 1975–1976. *Histoire de la France rurale*. 4 vols. Paris: Seuil.

Duggan, Lawrence. 1983. "Melchior von Meckau: A Missing Link in the Eck Zins-Disputes of 1514–1516?" *Archiv für Reformationsgeschichte*, 74: 25–37.

————. 1989. "Zur Bedeutung des spätmittelalterlichen Kreditsystems für die frühneuzeitliche deutsche Geschichte," in *Stände und Gesellschaft im alten Reich*, ed. Georg Schmidt. Stuttgart: Franz Steiner Verlag.

Economist. 1990. "Women's Value, Men's Worth." 10 November. P. 54.

Edwards, John. 1988. *The Jews in Christian Europe, 1400–1700*. London and New York: Routledge.

Elman, Peter. 1939. "Jewish Trade in Thirteenth Century England," *Historica judaica*, 1: 91–104.

Elvey, G. R., ed. 1975. *Luffield Priory Charters, Part II*. Welwyn Garden City: Buckinghamshire Record Society.

Embree, John F. 1969/1939. *Suye Mura: A Japanese Village*. Chicago: University of Chicago Press.

Emery, Richard. 1959. *The Jews of Perpignan in the Thirteenth Century*. New York: Columbia University Press.

Ennen, Edith. 1985. *Frauen im Mittelalter*. Munich: C. H. Beck.

Erler, Mary, and Maryanne Kowaleski, eds. 1988. *Women and Power in the Middle Ages*. Athens: University of Georgia Press.

Everett, Jana. 1989. "Incorporation versus Conflict: Lower Class Women, Collective Action, and the State in India," in *Women, the State and Development*, ed. Sue Ellen M. Charlton, Jana Everett, and Kathleen Staudt. Albany: State University of New York Press. Pp. 152–76.

Everett, Jana, and Mira Savara. 1985. "Institutional Credit for Female Petty Commodity Producers in India," in *Women Creating Wealth: Transforming Economic Development*, ed. R. Gallin and A. Spring. Washington, D.C.: Association for Women in Development. Pp. 143–48.

Faroqhi, Suraiya. 1984. *Towns and Townsmen of Ottoman Anatolia: Trade, Crafts and Food Production in an Urban Setting, 1520–1650*. Cambridge: Cambridge University Press.

————. 1987. *Men of Modest Substance: House Owners and House Property in Seventeenth-Century Ankara and Kayseri*. Cambridge: Cambridge University Press.

Feldman, Rayah. 1983. "Women's Groups and Women's Subordination: An Analysis of Policies Towards Rural Women in Kenya," *Review of African Political Economy*, nos. 27/28: 67–85.

Finley, Moses. 1952. *Studies in Land and Credit in Ancient Athens, 500–200 B.C.: The Horos-Inscriptions*. New Brunswick, N. J.: Rutgers University Press.

————. 1983. *Economy and Society in Ancient Greece*, ed. Brent D. Shaw and Richard D. Saller. Harmondsworth: Penguin.

Firth, Raymond. 1959. *Economics of the New Zealand Maori*. 2nd ed. Wellington: R. E. Owen, Government Printer.

————. 1965. *Primitive Polynesian Economy*. 2nd ed. London: Routledge and Kegan Paul.

————. 1966, 1946. *Malay Fishermen: Their Peasant Economy*. Hamden, Conn.: Archon Books.

Fischer, Henry. 1989. "Women in the Old Kingdom and the Heracleopolitan Period," in *Women's Earliest Records from Ancient Egypt and Western Asia*, ed. Barbara S. Lesko. Atlanta: Scholars Press. Pp. 5–30.

Forde, Daryll, and Mary Douglas. 1967. "Primitive Economics," in *Tribal and Peasant Economies*, ed. George Dalton. Garden City, N.Y.: Natural History Press. Pp. 13–28.

Forman, Shepard, and Joyce Riegelhaupt. 1970. "Market Place and Marketing System: Toward a Theory of Peasant Economic Integration," *Comparative Studies in Society and History*, 12: 188–212.

Fortmann, Louise. 1982. "Women's Work in a Communal Setting: The Tanzanian Policy of *Ujamaa*," in *Women and Work in Africa*, ed. Edna G. Bay. Boulder, Colo.: Westview Press. Pp. 191–205.

Fossier, Robert. 1988. *Peasant Life in the Medieval West*. Tr. J. Vale. Oxford: Basil Blackwell.

Foster, George, assisted by Gabriel Ospina. 1948. *Empire's Children: The People of Tzintzuntzan*. Smithsonian Institution: Institute of Social Anthropology, No. 6. Washington, D.C.: Smithsonian Institution.

Franklin, Peter. 1986. "Peasant Widows' 'Liberation' and Remarriage Before the Black Death," *Economic History Review*, 39: 186–204.

Franklin, Simon. 1985. "Literacy and Documentation in Early Medieval Russia," *Speculum*, 60: 1–38.

Fröhlich, Willy. 1982/1940. *The African Market System*. Tr. C. Good. Vancouver: Tantalus Research.

Gampel, Benjamin. 1989. *The Last Jews on Iberian Soil: Navarrese Jewry 1479/1498*. Berkeley: University of California Press.

Garfinkel, Irwin, and Sara McLanahan. 1986. *Single Mothers and Their Children: A New American Dilemma*. Washington, D.C.: Urban Institute Press.

Gasparri, Françoise. 1973–1974. "Les Juifs d'Orange (1311–1380) d'après les archives notariales," *Archives juives*, 10: 22–24.

Geertz, Clifford. 1961–1962. "The Rotating Credit Association: A 'Middle Rung' in Development," *Economic Development and Cultural Change*, 10: 241–63.

Geiges, Franziska. 1980. *Das Benedikterinnen-Kloster Frauenalb von den Anfängen bis zur Reformation*. Frankfurt-am-Main: Peter Lang.

Généstal, Robert. 1901. *Le Rôle des monastères comme établissements de crédit*. Paris: Arthur Rousseau.

Gerber, Haim. 1981. "Jews and Money-Lending in the Ottoman Empire," *Jewish Quarterly Review*, 72: 100–118.

Gilchrist, John Thomas. 1969. *The Church and Economic Activity During the Middle Ages*. London: Macmillan.

Gillin, John Philip. 1947. *Moche: A Peruvian Coastal Community*. Smithsonian Institution, Institute of Social Anthropology, No. 3. Washington, D.C.: Smithsonian Institution.

Goitein, S. D. 1967–1988. *A Mediterranean Society: The Jewish Communities of the Arab World as Portrayed in the Documents of the Cairo Geniza*. 5 vols. Berkeley: University of California Press.

Goldberg, P. J. P. 1986. "Female Labor, Service and Marriage in the Late Medieval Urban North," *Northern History*, 22: 18–38.

Goldsmith, Arthur, and Harvey Blustain. 1980. *Local Organization and Participation in Integrated Rural Development in Jamaica*. Ithaca, N. Y.: Rural Development Committee, Cornell University.

Gordon, Derek. 1989. "Women, Work and Social Mobility in Post-War Jamaica," in *Women and the Sexual Division of Labour*, ed. Keith Hart. Kingston: Consortium Graduate School of Social Sciences. Pp. 67–80.

Gordon, Elizabeth. 1980–1981. "An Analysis of the Impact of Labour Migration on the Lives of Women in Lesotho," *Journal of Development Studies*, 17: 59–76.

Gorman, Christine. 1990. "Giving Credit Where It's Overdue," *Time*, 135: 42.

Gough, Kathleen. 1981. *Rural Society in Southeast India*. Cambridge: Cambridge University Press.

Goveia, Elsa. 1965. *Slave Society in the British Leeward Islands at the End of the Eighteenth Century*. New Haven and London: Yale University Press.

Gullickson, Gay. 1986. *Spinners and Weavers of Auffay: Rural Industry and the Sexual Division of Labor in a French Village, 1750–1850*. Cambridge: Cambridge University Press.

Haagen, Paul. 1986. "Imprisonment for Debt in England and Wales." Unpublished Ph. D. dissertation, Princeton University.

Hafter, Daryl. 1985. "Artisans, Drudges, and the Problem of Gender in Pre-Industrial France," in *Science and Technology in Medieval Society*, ed. Pamela O. Long. Annals of the New York Academy of Sciences, 441. New York: New York Academy of Sciences. Pp. 71–87.

Hanawalt, Barbara. 1986. *The Ties That Bound: Peasant Families in Medieval England*. New York and Oxford: Oxford University Press.

Handler, Jerome. 1974. *The Unappropriated People: Freedmen in the Slave Society of Barbados*. Baltimore and London: Johns Hopkins University Press.

Handwerker, W. Penn. 1980. "Market Places, Travelling Traders, and Shops: Commercial Structural Variation in the Liberian Interior Prior to 1940," *African Economic History*, 9: 3–26.

Hansen, Karen. 1989. "The Black Market and Women Traders in Lusaka, Zambia," in *Women and the State in Africa*, ed. Jane L. Parpart and Kathleen A. Staudt. Boulder, Colo., and London: L. Rienner. Pp. 143–60.

Harris, Rivkah. 1989. "Independent Women in Ancient Mesopotamia," in *Women's Earliest Records from Ancient Egypt and Western Asia*, ed. Barbara S. Lesko. Atlanta: Scholars Press. Pp. 145–65.

Harriss, Barbara. 1980. "Money and Commodities, Monopoly and Competition," in *Borrowers and Lenders: Rural Financial Markets and Institutions in Developing Countries*, ed. J. Howell. London: Overseas Development Institute. Pp. 107–29.

Hart, Keith. 1970. "Small-Scale Entrepreneurs in Ghana and Development Planning," *Journal of Development Studies*, 6: 104–20.

———. 1982. *The Political Economy of West African Agriculture*. Cambridge: Cambridge University Press.

———. 1989a. "Introduction," in *Women and the Sexual Division of Labour*, ed. Keith Hart. Kingston: Consortium Graduate School of Social Sciences. Pp. 1–8.

———. 1989b. "The Sexual Division of Labour," in ibid., pp. 9–27.

Hay, Margaret. 1976. "Luo Women and Economic Change During the Colonial Period," in *Women in Africa: Studies in Social and Economic Change*, ed. Nancy J. Hafkin and Edna G. Bay. Stanford, Calif.: Stanford University Press. Pp. 87–109.

Henneman, John. 1971. *Royal Taxation in Fourteenth Century France: The Development of War Financing, 1322–1356*. Princeton, N.J.: Princeton University Press.

Herlihy, David. 1990. *Opera Muliebria: Women and Work in Medieval Europe*. New York: McGraw-Hill.

Herskovits, Melville. 1975/1937. *Life in a Haitian Valley*. New York: Knopf. Reprint New York: Octagon Books.

Herskovits, Melville, and Frances Herskovits. 1964/1947. *Trinidad Village*. New York: Knopf. Reprint New York: Octagon Books.

Hill, Polly. 1970a. *The Occupations of Migrants in Ghana*. Ann Arbor, Mich.: Museum of Anthropology, University of Michigan.

———. 1970b. *Studies in Rural Capitalism in West Africa*. Cambridge: Cambridge University Press.

———. 1972. *Rural Hausa: A Village and a Setting*. Cambridge: Cambridge University Press.

———. 1986. *Development Economics on Trial: The Anthropological Case for a Prosecution*. Cambridge: Cambridge University Press.

Hilton, Rodney. 1975. *The English Peasantry in the Later Middle Ages*. Oxford: Clarendon Press.

———. 1982. "Lords, Burgesses and Hucksters," *Past and Present*, no. 97, November 1982, 3–15.

———. 1992. *English and French Towns in Feudal Society: A Comparative Study*. Cambridge: Cambridge University Press.

Himmelstrand, Karin. 1990. "Can an Aid Bureaucracy Empower Women," in *Women, International Development, and Politics*, ed. Kathleen Staudt. Philadelphia: Temple University Press. Pp. 101–13.

Hodder, B. W., and U. I. Ukwu. 1969. *Markets in West Africa: Studies of Markets and Trade Among the Yoruba and Ibo*. Ibadan: Ibadan University Press.

Hodges, Richard. 1988. *Primitive and Peasant Markets*. Oxford: Basil Blackwell.

Hoffman, Philip T., Gilles Postel-Vinay, and Jean-Laurent Rosenthal. 1992. "Private Credit Markets in Paris, 1690–1840," *Journal of Economic History*, 52: 293–306.

Holderness, B. A. 1976. "Credit in English Rural Society Before the Nineteenth Century," *Agricultural History Review*, 24: 97–109.

———. 1981. "The Clergy as Money-Lenders in England, 1550–1700," in *Princes and Paupers in the English Church, 1500–1800*, ed. Rosemary O'Day and Felicity Heal. Leicester: Leicester University Press. Pp. 195–209.

———. 1984. "Widows in Pre-Industrial Society: An Essay upon Their Economic Functions," in *Land, Kinship and Life-Cycle*, ed. Richard M. Smith. Cambridge: Cambridge University Press. Pp. 423–42.

Hopkins, Anthony. 1973. *An Economic History of West Africa*. New York: Columbia University Press.

Howell, John, and Dale Adams. 1980. "Introduction," in *Borrowers and Lenders: Rural Financial Markets and Institutions in Developing Countries*, ed. John Howell. London: Overseas Development Institute. Pp. 1–12.

Huang, Ray. 1981. *1587, A Year of No Significance: The Ming Dynasty in Decline*. New Haven and London: Yale University Press.

Hudson, Kenneth. 1982. *Pawnbroking: An Aspect of British Social History*. London: Bodley Head.

Hufton, Olwen. 1975. "Women and the Family Economy in Eighteenth-Century France," *French Historical Studies*, 9: 1–22.

Hundert, Gershon. 1987. "The Role of the Jews in Commerce in Early Modern Poland-Lithuania," *Journal of European Economic History*, 16: 245–75.

Hutton, Diane. 1985. "Women in Fourteenth Century Shrewsbury," in *Women and Work in Pre-Industrial England*, ed. Lindsey Charles and Lorna Duffin. London: Croom Helm. Pp. 83–99.

Ianni, Octavio. 1984. "Social Organization and Alienation," in *Africa in Latin America: Essays on History, Culture, and Socialization*, ed. M. Moreno Fraginals. Tr. Leonor Blum. New York and Paris: Holmes and Meier. Pp. 38–57.

Ifeka, Caroline. 1989. "Women in Fisheries. Why Women Count: Prospects for Self-Reliant Fisheries Development in the South Pacific Compared to the Indian Ocean," in *Development and Social Change in the Pacific Islands*, ed. A. D. Couper. London and New York: Routledge. Pp. 89–114.

Irsigler, Franz. 1981. "Juden und Lombarden am Niederrhein im 14. Jahrhundert," in *Zur Geschichte der Juden im Deutschland des späten Mittelalters und der frühen Neuzeit*, ed. Alfred Haverkamp. Stuttgart: A. Hiersemann. Pp. 122–62.

Jacobsen, Grethe. 1983. "Women's Work and Women's Role: Ideology and Reality in Danish Urban Society," *Scandinavian Economic History Review*, 31: 3–20.

Jacoby, David. 1989. "New Evidence on Jewish Bankers in Venice and the Venetian Terraferma (c. 1450–1550)," in *The Mediterranean and the Jews: Banking, Finance and International Trade (XVI–XVIII Centuries)*, ed. Ariel Toaff and Simon Schwarzfuchs. Ramat-Gan: Bar-Ilan University Press. Pp. 151–78.

Jarck, Horst-Rüdiger, ed. 1982. *Urkundenbuch des Klosters Rinteln, 1224–1563*. Rinteln: Bosendahl.

Jarvis, Rupert. 1969. "Eighteenth-Century London Shipping," in *Studies in London History Presented to Philip Edmund Jones*, ed. A. E. J. Hollaender and William Kellaway. London: Hodder and Stoughton. Pp. 403–25.

Jeffrey, Peter. 1981. "A Bidding Prayer for Reconciliation," *Ephemerides liturgicae*, 95: 351–56.

Jehel, Georges. 1975. "Le Rôle des femmes et du milieu familial à Gênes dans les activités commerciales au cours de la première moitié du XIIIe siècle," *Revue d'histoire économique et sociale*, 53: 193–215.

Jemmali, Slaheddine. 1986. *Les Souks hébdomaires du Cap Bon (étude sociale et économique)*. Tunis: Maison Tunisienne de l'Édition.

Jenks, Stuart. 1978. "Judenverschuldung und Verfolgung von Juden im 14. Jahrhundert: Franken bis 1349," *Vierteljahrschrift für Sozial- und Wirtschaftsgeschichte*, 65: 309–55.

Jennings, Ronald. 1973. "Loans and Credit in Early 17th Century Ottoman Judicial Records: The Sharia Court of Anatolian Kayseri," *Journal of the Economic and Social History of the Orient*, 16: 168–216.

———. 1975. "Women in Early 17th Century Ottoman Judicial Records—The Sharia Court of Anatolian Kayseri," *Journal of the Economic and Social History of the Orient*, 18: 53–114.

———. 1978. "Zimmis (Non-Muslims) in Early 17th Century Ottoman Judicial Records: The Sharia Court of Anatolian Kayseri," *Journal of the Economic and Social History of the Orient*, 21: 225–93.

Johnny, Michael. 1985. *Informal Credit for Integrated Rural Development in Sierra Leone*. Hamburg: Verlag Weltarchiv.

Johnson, Cheryl. 1986. "Class and Gender: A Consideration of Yoruba Women During the Colonial Period," in *Women and Class in Africa*, ed. Claire Robertson and Iris Berger. New York and London: African Publishing. Pp. 237–54.

Jones, Norman. 1989. *God and the Moneylenders: Usury and Law in Early Modern England*. Oxford: Basil Blackwell.

Jordan, William Chester. 1978. "Jews on Top: Women and the Availability of Consumption Loans in Northern France in the Mid-Thirteenth Century," *Journal of Jewish Studies*, 29: 39–56.

———. 1979. "Jewish-Christian Relations in Mid-Thirteenth Century France: An Unpublished *Enquête* from Picardy," *Revue des études juives*, 138: 47–55.

———. 1981. "Communal Administration in France, 1257–1270: Problems Discovered and Solutions Imposed," *Revue belge de philologie et d'histoire*, 59: 1981.

———. 1983. "An Aspect of Credit in Picardy in the 1240s," *Revue des études juives*, 142: 141–52.

———. 1986. *From Servitude to Freedom: Manumission in the Sénonais in the Thirteenth Century*. Philadelphia: University of Pennsylvania Press.

———. 1988. "Women and Credit in the Middle Ages: Problems and Directions," *Journal of European Economic History*, 17: 33–62.

———. 1989. *The French Monarchy and the Jews: From Philip Augustus to the Last Capetians*. Philadelphia: University of Pennsylvania Press.

Karve, Irawati, and Hemalata Acharya. 1970. *The Role of Weekly Markets in the Tribal, Rural and Urban Setting*. Poona: S. M. Katre.

Kazgan, Gülten. 1981. "Labour Force Participation, Occupational Distribution, Educational Attainment and the Socio-Economic Status of Women in the Turkish Economy," in *Women in Turkish Society*, ed. N. Abadan-Unat. Leiden: Brill. Pp. 131–59.

Kendall, Laurel, and Mark Peterson. 1983. "'Traditional Korean Women'—A Reconsideration," in *Korean Women: View from the Inner Room*, ed. Laurel Kendall and Mark Peterson. New Haven, Conn.: East Rock Press. Pp. 5–21.

King, Peter. 1985. *The Finances of the Cistercian Order in the Fourteenth Century.* Kalamazoo, Mich.: Cistercian Publications.

Kirschenbaum, Aaron. 1985. "Jewish and Christian Theories of Usury in the Middle Ages," *Jewish Quarterly Review*, 75: 270–89.

Kirshner, Julius. 1978. *Pursuing Honor While Avoiding Sin: The Monte Delle Doti of Florence*. Milan: A. Guiffré.

Kist, Johannes. 1929. *Das Klarissenkloster in Nürnberg bis zum Beginn des 16. Jahrhunderts*. Nuremberg: Sebaldus-Verlag.

Kohn, Roger S. 1982. "Les Juifs de la France du Nord à travers les archives du Parlement de Paris (1359?-1394)," *Revue des études juives*, 141: 5–138.

———. 1988. *Les Juifs de la France du Nord dans la seconde moitié du XIVe siècle*. Louvain and Paris: E. Peeters.

Komlos, John, and Richard Landes. 1991. "Anachronistic Economics: Grain Storage in Medieval England," *Economic History Review*, 44: 36–45.

Koponen, Juhani. 1988. *People and Production in Late Precolonial Tanzania: History and Structures*. Jyväskylä: Finnish Society for Development Studies.

Kriegel, Maurice. 1979. *Les Juifs à la fin du moyen âge*. Paris: Hachette.

Krumme, Dwane. 1987. *Banking and the Plastic Card*. Washington, D.C.: American Bankers Association.

Kurtz, Donald. 1974. "Peripheral and Transitional Markets: The Aztec Case," *American Ethnologist*, 1: 685–705.

Lacey, Kay. 1985. "Women and Work in Fourteenth and Fifteenth Century London," in *Women and Work in Pre-Industrial England*, ed. Lindsey Charles and Lorna Duffin. London: Croom Helm. Pp. 24–82.

Ladipo, Patricia. 1981. "Developing Women's Cooperatives: An Experiment in Rural Nigeria," in *African Women in the Development Process*, ed. Nici Nelson. London: F. Cass. Pp. 123–36.

Langholm, Odd. 1984. *The Aristotelian Analysis of Usury*. Bergen and elsewhere: Universitetsforlaget.

Langlois, Charles-Victor. 1887. *Le Regne de Philippe III le Hardi*. Paris: Hachette.

Langmuir, Gavin. 1960. "'Judei nostri' and Capetian Legislation," *Traditio*, 16: 203–39.

Lary, N. M. 1986. *Dostoevsky and Soviet Film: Visions of Demonic Realism*. Ithaca, N. Y., and London: Cornell University Press.

Lavoie, Rodrigue. 1973. "Endettement et pauvreté en Provence d'après les listes de la justice comtale XIVe–XVe s.," *Provence historique*, 23: 201–16.

Lavrin, Asunción. 1973. "La Riqueza de los conventos de monjas en Nueva España: Estructura y evolución durante el siglo XVIII," *Cahiers des Ameriques latines*, 2 semester, 1973, 91–122.

———. 1979–1980. "La Congregación de San Pedro—una cofradía urbana del México colonial—1604–1730," *Historia mexicana*, 29: 562–601.

———. 1985. "El Capital eclesiástico y las elites sociales en Nueva España a fines del siglo XVIII," *Mexican Studies/Estudios mexicanos*, 1: 1–28.

Le Franc, Elsie. 1989. "Petty Trading and Labour Mobility: Higglers in the Kingston Metropolitan Area," in *Women and the Sexual Division of Labour*, ed. K. Hart. Kingston: Consortium Graduate School of Social Sciences. Pp. 99–132.

Le Goff, Jacques. 1986. *La Bourse et la vie: Économie et religion au moyen âge*. Paris: Hachette.

——. 1988. *Your Money or Your Life: Economy and Religion in the Middle Ages*. Tr. Patricia Ranum. New York: Zone Books.

Lehoux, Françoise. 1956. "Le Duc de Berri, les juifs et les Lombards," *Revue historique*, 215: 38–57.

Lelart, M. 1978. "L'Endettement du paysan et le crédit rural aux Philippines," *Études rurales*, no. 69: 51–79.

Lemire, Beverley. 1988. "Consumerism in Preindustrial and Early Industrial England: The Trade in Secondhand Clothes," *Journal of British Studies*, 27: 1–24.

Leroy, Béatrice. 1985. *The Jews of Navarre in the Late Middle Ages*. Tr. Jeffrey Green. Jerusalem: Magnes Press (Hebrew University).

Levin, Eve. 1983. "Women and Property in Medieval Novgorod: Dependence and Independence," *Russian History*, 10: 154–69.

Levy, Sandry. 1983. "Women and the Control of Property in Sixteenth-Century Muscovy," *Russian History*, 10: 201–12.

Lewis, Barbara. 1976. "The Limitations of Group Action among Entrepreneurs: The Market Women of Abidjan, Ivory Coast," in *Women in Africa: Studies in Social and Economic Change*, ed. Nancy J. Hafkin and Edna G. Bay. Stanford, Calif.: Stanford University Press.

——. 1982. "Women in Development Planning: Advocacy, Institutionalization and Implementation," in *Perspectives on Power: Women in Africa, Asia, and Latin America*, ed. Jean F. O'Barr. Durham, N. C.: Center for International Studies, Duke University. Pp. 102–18.

——. 1984. "The Impact of Development Policies on Women," in *African Women South of the Sahara*, ed. Margaret Jean Hay and Sharon Stichter. London and New York: Longman. Pp. 170–87.

Lewis, Patricia. 1979. "Mortgages in the Bordelais and Bazadais," *Viator*, 10: 23–38.

Lipman, Vivian D. 1967. *The Jews of Medieval Norwich*. London: Jewish Historical Society of England.

Little, Kenneth. 1973. *African Women in Towns: An Aspect of Africa's Social Revolution*. Cambridge: Cambridge University Press.

——. 1975. "Some Methodological Considerations in the Study of African Women's Urban Roles," *Urban Anthropology*, 4: 107–21.

——. 1980. *The Sociology of Urban Women's Image in African Literature*. London: Macmillan.

Little, Lester. 1971. "Pride Goes Before Avarice: Social Change and the Vices in Latin Christendom," *American Historical Review*, 76: 16–49.

1978. *Religious Poverty and the Profit Economy in Medieval Europe*. London: P. Elek; Ithaca, N.Y.: Cornell University Press.

Loeb, Isadore. 1884. "Deux Livres de commerce du commencement du XIVe siècle," *Revue des études juives*, 8: 161–96.

Loevinson, Ermanno. 1932a. "La Concession de banques de prêts aux juifs par les

Papes des seizième et dix-septième siècles," part I, *Revue des études juives*, 92: 1–30.

———. 1932b. Part II. Ibid. 93: 27–52

———. 1932c. Part III. Ibid. 93: 157–78.

———. 1933a. Part IV. Ibid. 94: 57–72.

———. 1933b. Part V. Ibid. 94: 167–83.

———. 1933c. Part VI. Ibid. 95: 23–43.

Lopez, Robert. 1971. *The Commercial Revolution of the Middle Ages, 950–1350*. Englewood Cliffs, N.J.: Prentice-Hall.

Lowenthal, David. 1990. "Degradation and Celebration: Caribbean Environments and Indigenes," *Journal of Historical Geography*, 16: 223–29.

Lüthy, Herbert. 1959–1961. *La Banque protestante en France de la Révocation de l'Édit de Nantes à la Révolution*. 2 vols. Paris: SEVPEN.

Luzzatto, Gino. 1902. *I Banchieri ebrei in Urbino nell'età ducale*. Padua: Società Cooperativa Tipografica.

McAlister, E. Ray. 1975. *An Empirical Analysis of Retail Revolving Credit*. West Lafayette, Ind.: Credit Research Center, Purdue University.

MacGaffey, Janet. 1986. "Women and Class Formation in a Dependent Economy; Kisangani Entrepreneurs," in *Women and Class in Africa*, ed. Claire Robertson and Iris Berger. New York and London: Africana Publishing. Pp. 161–77.

———. 1988. "Evading Male Control: Women in the Second Economy in Zaire," in *Patriarchy and Class: African Women in the Home and Workplace*, ed. Sharon B. Stichter and Jane L. Parpart. Boulder, Colo.: Westview Press. Pp. 161–76.

McGuire, Brian. 1982. *The Cistercians in Denmark*. Kalamazoo, Mich.: Cistercian Publications.

McIntosh, Marjorie. 1986. *Autonomy and Community: The Royal Manor of Havering, 1200–1500*. Cambridge: Cambridge University Press.

———. 1988. "Money Lending on the Periphery of London, 1300–1600," *Albion*, 20: 557–71.

McLaughlin, T. 1939. "The Teaching of the Canonists on Usury," *Medieval Studies*, 1: 81–147.

———. 1940. Ibid., 2: 1–22.

Madrigal, Moon. 1979. *The Role of Women in Korean Society with Emphasis on the Economic System*. Palo Alto, Cal.: R & E Research Associates.

Mandell, Lewis, and Neil Murphy. 1976. *Bank Cards*. Washington, D.C.: American Institute of Banking.

Marsh, Robin. 1983. *Development Strategies in Rural Colombia: The Case of Caquetá*. Los Angeles: Latin American Center, University of California-Los Angeles.

Martin, Lawrence. 1979. "The Earliest Versions of the Latin *Somniale Danielis*," *Manuscripta*, 23: 131–41.

Massiah, Joycelin. 1984. "Indicators of Women in Development: A Preliminary Framework for the Caribbean," in *Women, Work and Development*, ed. Margaret Gilland and Joycelin Massiah. Cave Hill, Barbados: Institute for Social and Economic Research (Eastern Caribbean), University of West Indies. Pp. 41–129.

———. 1986. "Postscript: The Utility of WCIP Research in Social Policy Formation," *Social and Economic Studies*, 35: 157–201.

Mayhew, N. J. 1987. "Money and Prices in England from Henry II to Edward III," *Agricultural History Review*, 35: 121–32.

Menkes, Fred. 1971. "Une communauté juive en Provence au XIVe siècle: Étude d'un groupe social," *Le Moyen Age*, 77: 277–303, 417–50.

Mertes, Kate. 1988. *The English Noble Household 1250 to 1600: Good Governance and Politic Rule*. Oxford: Basil Blackwell.

Mintz, Sidney. 1960. "A Tentative Typology of Eight Haitian Marketplaces," *Revista de ciencias sociales*, 4: 15–57.

——. 1971. "Men, Women and Trade," *Comparative Studies in Society and History*, 13: 247–69.

——. 1974a. *Caribbean Transformations*. Chicago: Aldine.

——. 1974b. "Les Rôles économiques et la tradition culturelle," in *La Femme de couleur en Amérique latine*, ed. Roger Bastide. Paris: Éditions Anthropos. Pp. 115–48.

——. 1978. "Caribbean Marketplaces and Caribbean History," *Nova Americana*, 1: 333–44.

——. 1984. "Africa *of* Latin America: An Unguarded Reflection," in *Africa in Latin America: Essays on History, Culture, and Socialization*, ed. M. Moreno Fraginals. Tr. L. Blum. New York: Holmes and Meier. Pp. 286–305.

Miracle, Marvin, Diane Miracle,, and Laurie Cohen. 1979–1980. "Informal Savings Mobilization in Africa," *Economic Development and Cultural Change*, 28: 700–724.

Moen, Elizabeth, Elise Boulding, Jane Lillydahl, and Risa Palm. 1981. *Women and the Social Costs of Economic Development: Two Colorado Case Studies*. Boulder, Colo.: Westview Press.

Moreau, Marthe. 1988. *L'Âge d'or des religieuses: Monastères féminins du Languedoc méditerranéen au moyen âge*. Cahors: Presses du Languedoc.

Morenzoni, Franco. 1992. "Les Prêteurs d'argent et leurs clients dans le Valais savoyard à la veille de la peste noire. La Casane de Sembrancher ent 1347," *Schweizerische Zeitschrift für Geschichte*, 42: 1–27.

Morrissey, Marietta. 1989. *Slave Women in the New World: Gender Stratification in the Caribbean*. Lawrence: University Press of Kansas.

Mundill, Robin. 1991. "Lumbard and Son: The Businesses and Debtors of Two Jewish Moneylenders in Late Thirteenth-Century England," *Jewish Quarterly Review*, 82: 137–70.

Mundy, John. 1982. "Urban Society and Culture: Toulouse and Its Region," in *Renaissance and Renewal in the Twelfth Century*, ed. Robert L. Benson and Giles Constable. Cambridge, Mass.: Harvard University Press. Pp. 229–47.

——. 1987. "Les Femmes à Toulouse au temps des Cathares," *Annales: ESC*, 42: 117–34.

Muntemba, Maud. 1982. "Women and Agricultural Change in the Railway Region of Zambia: Dispossession and Counterstrategies, 1930–1970," in *Women and Work in Africa*, ed. Edna G. Bay. Boulder, Colo.: Westview Press. Pp. 83–103.

Nahon, Gérard. 1969. "Le Crédit et les juifs dans la France du XIIIe siècle," *Annales: ESC*, 24: 1121–48.

Nelson, Benjamin. 1969. *The Idea of Usury: From Tribal Brotherhood to Universal Otherhood*. 2nd ed. Chicago: University of Chicago Press.

Nelson, Nici. 1979. "How Women and Men Get By: The Sexual Division of Labour in the Informal Sector of a Nairobi Squatter Settlement," in *Casual Work and Poverty in Third World Cities*, ed. Ray Bromley and Chris Gerry. Chichester and New York: Wiley. Pp. 283–302.

New York Times. 1990. "Credit as a Human Right." 2 April. P. A 17.

Nguyen Van Vinh. 1949. *Savings and Mutual Lending Societies* (Ho) (typescript on deposit, Firestone Library, Princeton University).

Nicholas, David. 1985. *The Domestic Life of a Medieval City: Women, Children, and the Family in Fourteenth-Century Ghent*. Lincoln and London: University of Nebraska Press.

Nichols, Nancy. 1989. "'How's Your Bank, Honey?'" *Ms.*, 17: 142.

Noonan, John T. 1957. *The Scholastic Analysis of Usury*. Cambridge, Mass.: Harvard University Press.

Norton, Ann, and Richard Syzmanski. 1975. "The Internal Marketing Systems of Jamaica," *Geographical Review*, 65: 461–75.

Nwihim, Martha. 1983. "Economic Role Played by Nigerian Women," in *The Role of Women in the Process of Development*, ed. G. Ssenkoloto (Cahiers no. 7). Douala: Institut Panafricain pour le Développement. Pp. 113–18.

Obbo, Christine. 1980. *African Women: Their Struggle for Economic Independence*. London: Zed Press.

Ocharo, A. O. 1975. "The Disparity and Relationship of Rural Markets in East Kasipul, South Nyanza, Kenya," in *Geographical Studies on Rural Markets in East Africa from Makerere*, ed. B. Langlands. Kampala: Department of Geography, Makerere University. Pp. 7–40.

Ortiz, Sutti. 1967. "Colombian Rural Market Organisation: An Exploratory Model," *Man*, 2: 393–414.

Parpart, Jane L., ed. 1989. *Women and Development in Africa: Comparative Perspectives*. Lanham, Md.: University Press of America.

Pauly, August Friedrich von. 1894–. *Realencyclopädie der classischen Alterthumswissenschaft*. 34 vols. and 15 supplementary vols. to date. Stuttgart: Metzler.

Pellow, Deborah. 1978. "Work and Autonomy: Women in Accra," *American Ethnologist*, 5: 770–85.

Penn, Simon. 1987. "Female Wage-Earners in Late Fourteenth-Century England," *Agricultural History Review*, 35: 1–15.

Per-Lee, Dianne. 1984. "Street Vendors," in *Women and Work in India: Continuity and Change*, ed. Joyce Lebra, Joy Paulson, and Jana Everett. New Delhi: Promilla. Pp. 184–200.

Piel, Margaret. 1979. "Host Reactions: Aliens in Ghana," in *Strangers in African Societies*, ed. William A. Shack and Elliott P. Skinner. Berkeley: University of California Press. Pp. 123–40.

Pirenne, Henri. 1937. *Economic and Social History of Medieval Europe*. Tr. I. Clegg. New York: Harcourt, Brace, and World.

Poliakov, Léon. 1977. *Jewish Bankers and the Holy See: From the Thirteenth to the Seventeenth Century*. Tr. Miriam Kochan. London: Routledge and Kegan Paul.

Pollak-Eltz, Angelina. 1974. "La Femme de couleur au Vénézuela," in *La Femme de couleur en Amérique latine*, ed. Roger Bastide. Paris: Éditions Anthropos. Pp. 221–46.

Pollock, Frederick, and Frederic William Maitland. 1968/1898. *The History of English Law Before the Time of Edward I*. 2nd ed. 2 vols. Cambridge: Cambridge University Press.

Postan, Michael. 1927–1928. "Credit in Medieval Trade," *Economic History Review*, 1: 234–61.

Powell, James. Unpub. "The Role of Women in the Fifth Crusade."

Power, Eileen. 1975. *Medieval Women*. ed. M. M. Postan. Cambridge: Cambridge University Press.

Powicke, Maurice. 1961. *The Loss of Normandy, 1189–1204: Studies in the History of the Angevin Empire*. 2nd ed. Manchester: Manchester University Press.

Prior, Mary. 1990. "Wives and Wills 1558–1700," in *English Rural Society, 1500–1800: Essays in Honour of Joan Thirsk*, ed. John Chartres and David Hey. Cambridge: Cambridge University Press. Pp. 201–25.

Prochaska, David. 1987. "Cagayous of Algiers." Unpublished Davis Seminar Paper, Princeton University.

———. 1990. *Making Algeria French: Colonialism in Bône, 1870–1920*. Cambridge: Cambridge University Press.

Pullan, Brian. 1987. "Jewish Moneylending in Venice: From Private Enterprise to Public Service," in *Gli Ebrei e Venezia: secoli XIV–XVIII*, ed. Gaetano Cozzi. Milan: Edizioni Comunità. Pp. 671–86.

Queller, Donald, and Thomas Madden. Unpub. "Father of the Bride: Fathers, Daughters, and Dowries in Late Medieval and Early Renaissance Venice."

Raban, Sandra. 1982. *Mortmain Legislation and the English Church, 1279–1500*. Cambridge: Cambridge University Press.

Rabelais, François. [1955]. *The Histories of Gargantua and Pantagruel*. Tr. J. Cohen. Harmondsworth: Penguin.

Reichel-Dolmatoff, Inès. 1974. "Aspects de la vie de la femme noire dans le passé et de nos jours en Colombie (côte atlantique)," in *La Femme de couleur en Amérique latine*, ed. Roger Bastide. Paris: Éditions Anthropos. Pp. 247–65.

Ravensdale, Jack. 1984. "Population Changes and the Transfer of Customary Land on a Cambridgeshire Manor in the Fourteenth Century," in *Land, Kinship and the Life-Cycle*, ed. Richard M. Smith. Cambridge: Cambridge University Press. Pp. 197–225.

Ravid, Benjamin. 1989. "An Autobiographical Memorandum by Daniel Rodriga, *Inventore* of the *Scala* of *Spalato*," in *The Mediterranean and the Jews: Banking, Finance and International Trade (XVI–XVIII Centuries)*, ed. Ariel Toaff and Simon Schwarzfuchs. Ramat-Gan: Bar-Ilan University Press. Pp. 189–213.

Reyerson, Kathryn. 1985. *Business, Banking and Finance in Medieval Montpellier*. Toronto: Pontifical Institute of Mediaeval Studies.

———. 1986. "Women in Business in Medieval Montpellier," in *Women and Work in Preindustrial Europe*, ed. Barbara A. Hanawalt. Bloomington: Indiana University Press. Pp. 117–44.

Richardson, Henry. 1960. *English Jewry Under the Angevin Kings*. London: Methuen.

Riemer, Eleanor. 1985. "Women, Dowries, and Capital Investment in Thirteenth Century Siena," in *The Marriage Bargain: Women and Dowries in European History*, ed. Marion A. Kaplan. New York: Haworth Press. Pp. 59–79.

Rigg, James, ed. 1905–1972. *Calendar of the Plea Rolls of the Exchequer of the Jews.* 4 vols. London: Dawson.

Roach, Andrew. 1986. "The Cathar Economy," *Reading Medieval Studies*, 12: 51–71.

Robertson, Claire. 1976. "Ga Women and Socioeconomic Change in Accra, Ghana," in *Women in Africa: Studies in Social and Economic Change*, ed. Nancy J. Hafkin and Edna G. Bay. Stanford, Calif.: Stanford University Press. Pp. 113–33.

———. 1984. "Women in the Urban Economy," in *African Women South of the Sahara*, ed. Margaret Jean Hay and Sharon Stichter. London and New York: Longman. Pp. 33–50.

Robins, Gay. 1989. "Some Images of Women in New Kingdom Art and Literature," in *Women's Earliest Records from Ancient Egypt and Western Asia*, ed. Barbara S. Lesko. Atlanta: Scholars Press. Pp. 105–21.

Rosen, Josef. 1987. "Two Municipal Accounts: Frankfurt and Basel in 1428," *Journal of European Economic History*, 16: 363–88.

Rosenthal, Gilbert, ed. 1962. *Banking and Finance Among Jews in Renaissance Italy: A Critical Edition of* The Eternal Life (Haye Olam) *by Yehiel Nissim da Pisa.* New York: Bloch.

Ross, Charles, ed. 1959. *Chartulary of St. Mark's Hospital, Bristol.* Bristol: Bristol Record Society.

Ross, Ellen. Unpub. Section on "Pawning and Power" from unpublished manuscript on "Love and Labor in Outcast London."

Rostovtzeff, Michael. 1941. *The Social and Economic History of the Hellenistic World.* 3 vols. Oxford: Clarendon Press.

———. 1957. *The Social and Economic History of the Roman Empire.* 2nd ed. 2 vols. Oxford: Clarendon Press.

Roth, Cecil. 1964. *A History of the Jews in England.* 3rd ed. Oxford: Clarendon Press.

Rubin, Miri. 1987. *Charity and Community in Medieval Cambridge.* Cambridge: Cambridge University Press.

Sabean, David. 1990. *Property, Production, and Family in Neckarhausen, 1700–1870.* Cambridge: Cambridge University Press.

Safa, Helen. 1986. "Economic Autonomy and Sexual Equality in Caribbean Society," *Social and Economic Studies*, 35: 1–21.

———. 1990. "Women and Industrialisation in the Caribbean," in *Women, Employment and the Family in the International Division of Labour*, ed. Sharon Stichter and Jane L. Parpart. London: Macmillan. Pp. 72–97.

Sahlins, Marshall. 1972. *Stone Age Economics.* Chicago: Aldine-Atherton.

Samsonowicz, Henryk. 1988. "Les Villes d'Europe centrale à la fin du moyen âge," *Annales: ESC*, 43: 173–84.

Saul, Mahir. 1981. "Beer, Sorghum and Women: Production for the Market in Rural Upper Volta," *Africa: Journal of the International African Institute*, 51: 746–64.

——. 1987. "The Organization of a West African Grain Market," *American Anthropologist*, 89: 74–95.

Saulniers, Suzanne Smith, and Cathy Rakowski. 1977. *Women in the Development Process: A Select Bibliography on Women in Sub-Saharan Africa and Latin America*. Austin: Institute of Latin American Studies, University of Texas.

Schildkrout, Enid. 1979. "The Ideology of Regionalism in Ghana," in *Strangers in African Societies*, ed. William A. Shack and Elliott P. Skinner. Berkeley: University of California Press. Pp. 183–207.

——. 1982. "Dependence and Autonomy: The Economic Activities of Secluded Hausa Women in Kano, Nigeria," in *Women and Work in Africa*, ed. Edna G. Bay. Boulder, Colo.: Westview Press. Pp. 55–81.

Schilperoort, Gijsbert. 1933. *Le Commerçant dans la littérature française du moyen âge (caractère, vie, position sociale)*. Groningen and The Hague: Wolters.

Schneider, Reinhard. 1975. "Güter- und Gelddepositen in Zisterzienserklöstern," *Zisterzienser-Studien*, 1: 97–126.

Schuster, Ilsa. 1982. "Marginal Lives: Conflict and Contradiction in the Position of Female Traders in Lusaka, Zambia," in *Women and Work in Africa*, ed. Edna G. Bay. Boulder, Colo.: Westview Press. Pp. 105–26.

Schwarzfuchs, Simon. 1989. "Quand Commença le déclin de l'industrie textile des juifs de Salonique," in *The Mediterranean and the Jews: Banking, Finance and International Trade (XVI–XVIII Centuries)*, ed. Ariel Toaff and Simon Schwarzfuchs. Ramat-Gan: Bar-Ilan University Press. Pp. 215–35.

Schwimmer, Brian. 1979. "Market Structure and Social Organization in a Ghanaian Marketing System," *American Ethnologist*, 6: 682–701.

Searle, Eleanor. 1974. *Lordship and Community: Battle Abbey and Its Banlieu, 1066–1538*. Toronto: Pontifical Institute of Mediaeval Studies.

Seduro, Vladimir. 1977. *Dostoevsky in Russian and World Theatre*. North Quincy, Mass.: Christopher Publishing House.

Segre, Renata. 1986. *The Jews in Piedmont*, I: *1297–1582*. Jerusalem: Israel Academy of Sciences and Humanities.

Shahar, Shulamith. 1983. *The Fourth Estate: A History of Women in the Middle Ages*. Tr. C. Galai. London and New York: Methuen.

Shatzmiller, Joseph. 1989. "Travelling in the Mediterranean in 1563: The Testimony of Eliahu of Pesaro," in *The Mediterranean and the Jews: Banking, Finance and International Trade (XVI–XVIII Centuries)*, ed. Ariel Toaff and Simon Schwarzfuchs. Ramat-Gan: Bar-Ilan University Press. Pp. 237–48.

——. 1990. *Shylock Reconsidered: Jews, Moneylending, and Medieval Society*. Berkeley: University of California Press.

Shaw, R. Paul. 1981. "Women's Employment in the Arab World," *Development and Change*, 12: 237–71.

Shipley, Neal. 1976. "Thomas Sutton: Tudor-Stuart Moneylender," *Business History Review*, 50: 456–76.

Shmuelevitz, Aryeh. 1984. *The Jews of the Ottoman Empire in the Late Fifteenth and the Sixteenth Centuries: Administrative, Economic, Legal and Social Relations as Reflected in the Responsa*. Leiden: Brill.

Shohet, David. 1974/1931. *The Jewish Court in the Middle Ages*. New York: Commanday-Roth. Reprint New York: Hermon Press.

Sidebotham, Steven. 1986. *Roman Economic Policy in the Erythra Thalassa: 30 B.C.–A.D. 217*. Leiden: Brill.

Simonsohn, Shlomo. 1977. *History of the Jews in the Duchy of Mantua*. Jerusalem: Kiryath Sepher.

———. 1982–1986. *The Jews in the Duchy of Milan*. 4 vols. Jerusalem: Israel Academy of Sciences and Humanities.

Simpson, George. 1942. "Sexual and Familial Institutions in Northern Haiti," *American Anthropologist*, 44: 655–74.

Skinner, G. William. 1964. "Marketing and Social Structure in Rural China, Part I," *Journal of Asian Studies*, 24: 3–43.

Snape, Robert. 1926. *English Monastic Finances in the Later Middle Ages*. Cambridge: Cambridge University Press.

Somers, J. 1980. "Bijdrage tot de Geschiedenis van de Lombarden in Brabant tijdens de late Middeleeuwen." Master's thesis, Catholic University of Louvain.

Sorensen, Clark. 1983. "Women, Men; Inside, Outside: The Division of Labor in Rural Central Korea," in *Korean Women: View from the Inner Room*, ed. Laurel Kendall and Mark Peterson. New Haven, Conn.: East Rock Press. Pp. 63–79.

Staudt, Kathleen. 1982. "Women Farmers and Inequities in Agricultural Services," in *Women and Work in Africa*, ed. Edna G. Bay. Boulder, Colo.: Westview Press. Pp. 207–24.

———. 1986. "Stratification: Implications for Women's Politics," in *Women and Class in Africa*, ed. Claire Robertson and Iris Berger. New York and London: Africana Publishing. Pp. 197–215.

Stichter, Sharon. 1984. "Appendix: Some Selected Statistics on African Women," in *African Women South of the Sahara*, ed. Margaret Jean Hay and Sharon Stichter. London and New York: Longman. Pp. 188–94.

Stirrat, R. L. 1989. "Money, Men and Women," in *Money and the Morality of Exchange*, ed. J. Parry and M. Bloch. Cambridge: Cambridge University Press. Pp. 94–116.

Stow, Kenneth. 1981. "Papal and Royal Attitudes Toward Jewish Lending in the Thirteenth Century," *AJSreview*, 6: 161–83.

———. 1987. "The Jewish Family in the Rhineland in the High Middle Ages: Form and Function," *American Historical Review*, 92: 1085–1110.

Stow, Kenneth, and Sandra Stow. 1986. "Donne ebree a Roma nell'età de ghetto: affetto, dipendenza, autonomia," *Rassegna mensile di Israel*, 52: 63–116.

Sudarkasa, Niara. 1973. *Where Women Work: A Study of Yoruba Women in the Marketplace and in the Home*. Ann Arbor: University of Michigan Press.

Swain, John T. 1986. *Industry Before the Industrial Revolution: North-East Lancashire, c. 1500–1640*. Manchester: Manchester University Press.

Swanson, Heather. 1989. *Medieval Artisans: An Urban Class in Late Medieval England*. Oxford: Basil Blackwell.

Szanton, M. Christina. 1982. "Women and Men in Iloilo, Philippines: 1903–1970," in *Women of Southeast Asia*, ed. Penny Van Esterik. Dekalb, Ill.: Center for Southeast Asia Studies, Northern Illinois University. Pp. 124–53.

Tallan, Cheryl. 1991. "Medieval Jewish Widows: Their Control of Resources," *Jewish History*, 5: 63–74.

Taplin, Ruth. 1989. *Economic Development and the Role of Women: An Interdisciplinary Approach*. Aldershot: Gower.

Tawney, Richard. 1925. "Introduction," in Thomas Wilson, *A Discourse upon Usury*. New York: Harcourt, Brace. Pp. 1–172.

Taylor, George. 1962. "The Paris Bourse on the Eve of the Revolution, 1781–1789," *American Historical Review*, 67: 951–77.

Tebbutt, Melanie. 1983. *Making Ends Meet: Pawn Broking and Working-Class Credit*. New York: St. Martin's Press.

Thiriot, G. 1926. *Les Carmélites de Metz*. Metz: Imprimerie Lorraine.

Tillotson, John. 1989. *Marrick Priory: A Nunnery in Late Medieval Yorkshire*. Borthwick Papers, No. 75.

Tinker, Irene. 1990. "The Making of a Field: Advocates, Practitioners, and Scholars," in *Persistent Inequalities: Women and World Development*, ed. Irene Tinker. New York: Oxford University Press. Pp. 27–53.

Toaff, Ariel. 1979. *The Jews in Medieval Assisi 1305–1487: A Social and Economic History of a Small Jewish Community in Italy*. Florence: L. S. Olschki.

———. 1983. "Gli Ebrei romani e il commercio del denaro nei comuni dell'Italia centrale alla fine del duecento," in *Italia Judaica*. Rome. Pp. 183–96.

Toch, Michael. 1982. "Geld und Kredit in einer spätmittelalterlichen Landschaft: Zu einem unbeachteten hebräischen Schuldenregister aus Niederbayern (1329–1332)," *Deutsches Archiv*, 38: 499–550.

Todd, Barbara. 1990. "Freebench and Free Enterprise: Widows and Their Property in Two Berkshire Villages," in *English Rural Society, 1500–1800: Essays in Honour of Joan Thirsk*, ed. John Chartres and David Hey. Cambridge: Cambridge University Press. Pp. 175–200.

Udovitch, Abraham. 1967. "Credit as a Means of Investment in Medieval Islamic Trade," *Journal of the American Oriental Society*, 87: 260–64.

Udry, Christopher. 1990. "Credit Markets in Northern Nigeria: Credit as Insurance in a Rural Economy," *World Bank Economics Review*, 4: 251–69.

Uitz, Erika. 1986. "Die Frau im Berufsleben der spätmittelalterlichen Stadt, untersucht am Beispiel von Städten auf dem Gebiet der Deutschen Demokratischen Republik," in *Frau und spätmittelalterlicher Alltag*. Vienna: Verlag der Österreichischen Akademie der Wissenschaften. Pp. 439–73.

Ulrich, Laurel. 1988. "Martha Ballard and Her Girls: Women's Work in Eighteenth-Century Maine," in *Work and Labor in Early America*, ed. Stephen Innes. Chapel Hill and London: University of North Carolina Press. Pp. 70–105.

———. 1990. *A Midwife's Tale: The Life of Martha Ballard, Based on Her Diary, 1785–1812*. New York: Knopf.

United Nations. 1972. Economic Commission for Africa, "Women: The Neglected Human Resource for African Development," *Canadian Journal of African Studies*, 6: 359–70.

Unwin, Tim. 1981. "Rural Marketing in Medieval Nottinghamshire," *Journal of Historical Geography*, 7: 231–51.

Usilton, Larry. 1980. "Edward I's Exploitation of the Corrody System," *American Benedictine Review*, 31: 222–36.

Valois, Noël. 1908. "Un Plaidoyer du XIVe siècle en faveur des Cisterciens," *Bibliothèque de l'École de chartes*, 69: 352–68.

Vanja, Christina. 1984. *Besitz- und Sozialgeschichte der Zisterzienserinnenklöster Caldern und Georgenberg und des Prämonstratenserinnenstiftes Hachborn in Hessen im späten Mittelalter*. Darmstadt and Marburg: Hessische Historische Kommission.

———. 1986. "Frauen im Dorf: Ihre Stellung unter besonderer Berücksichtigung landgräflich-hessischer Quellen des späten Mittelalters," *Zeitschrift für Agrargeschichte und Agrarsoziologie*, 34: 147–59.

Vassberg, David. 1984. *Land and Society in Golden Age Castile*. Cambridge: Cambridge University Press.

Vassoigne, Yolène de. 1974. "La Femme dans la société antillaise 'française'," in *La Femme de couleur en Amérique latine*, ed. Roger Bastide. Paris: Éditions Anthropos. Pp. 193–209.

Veenhof, K. R. 1972. *Aspects of Old Assyrian Trade and Its Terminology*. Leiden: Brill.

Veinstein, Gilles. 1987. "Une Communauté ottomane: les juifs d'Avlonya (Valona) dans la deuxième moitié du XVI siècle," in *Gli Ebrei e Venezia: secoli XIV – XVIII*, ed. Gaetano Cozzi. Milan: Edizioni Comunità. Pp. 781–828.

Velde, François R., and David R. Weir. 1992. "The Financial Market and Government Debt Policy in France, 1746–1793," *Journal of Economic History*, 52: 1–39.

Vélez-Ibañez, Carlos. 1983. *Bonds of Mutual Trust: The Cultural Systems of Rotating Credit Associations among Urban Mexicans and Chicanos*. New Brunswick, N. J.: Rutgers University Press.

Vercruijsse, Emile. 1984. *The Penetration of Capitalism: A West African Case Study*. London: Zed Press.

Verdon, Jean. 1986. "La Vie quotidienne de la femme en France au bas moyen âge," in *Frau und spätmittelalterlicher Alltag*. Vienna: Verlag der Osterreichischen Akademie der Wissenschaften. Pp. 325–86.

Ville, Simon. 1987. *English Shipowning During the Industrial Revolution: Michael Henley and Son, London Shipowners, 1770–1830*. Manchester: Manchester University Press.

Vincent, Jeanne-Françoise. 1966. *Femmes africaines en milieu urbain*. Paris: Office de la Recherche Scientifique et Technique Outre-Mer.

Von der Mehden, Fred. 1968. *Religion and Nationalism in Southeast Asia*. Madison: University of Wisconsin Press.

Wagner, Heinrich, ed. 1987. *Regesten der Zisterzienserabtei Bildhausen, 1158–1525*. Würzburg: F. Schoningh.

Wales, Tim. 1984. "Poverty, Poor Relief and the Life Cycle: Some Evidence from Seventeenth-Century Norfolk," in *Land, Kinship and Life-Cycle*, ed. Richard M. Smith. Cambridge: Cambridge University Press.

Warner, John. 1976. "Survey of the Market System in the Nochixtlán Valley and the Mixteca Alta," in *Markets in Oaxaca*, ed. Scott Cook and Martin Diskin. Austin and London: University of Texas Press. Pp. 107–31.

Weill, G. 1966. "Les Juifs dans le Barrois et la Meuse du moyen âge à nos jours," *Revue des études juives*, 125: 287–301.

Weisser, Michael. 1987. "Rural Crisis and Rural Credit in XVIIth-Century Castile," *Journal of European Economic History*, 16: 297–313.

Werbner, Pnina. 1988. "Taking and Giving: Working Women and Female Bonds in a Pakistani Immigrant Neighbourhood," in *Enterprising Women: Ethnicity, Economy, and Gender Relations*, Sallie Westwood and Parminder Bhachu. London and New York: Routledge. Pp. 177–202.

Wernham, Monique. 1979. "La Communauté juive de Salon-de-Provence d'après les actes notariés." Thèse de doctorat de 3ème cycle, University of Aix-en-Provence.

Wharton, C. R. 1962. "Marketing, Merchandising, and Moneylending: A Note on Middleman Monopsony in Malaya," *Malayan Economic Review*, 7: 24–44.

White, E. Frances. 1982. "Women, Work, and Ethnicity: The Sierra Leone Case," in *Women and Work in Africa*, ed. Edna G. Bay. Boulder, Colo.: Westview Press. Pp. 19–33.

———. 1987. *Sierra Leone's Settler Women Traders: Women on the Afro-European Frontier*. Ann Arbor: University of Michigan Press.

White, Louise. 1988. "Domestic Labor in a Colonial City: Prostitution in Nairobi, 1900–1952," in *Patriarchy and Class: African Women in the Home and Workplace*, ed. Sharon Stichter and Jane L. Parpart. Boulder, Colo.: Westview Press. Pp. 139–60

Whyte, Robert, and Pauline Whyte. 1982. *The Women of Rural Asia*. Boulder, Colo.: Westview Press.

Wiesner [Wood], Merry. 1981. "Paltry Peddlers or Essential Merchants? Women in the Distributive Trades in Early Modern Nuremberg," *Sixteenth Century Journal*, 12: 3–13.

Wikan, Unni. 1982. *Behind the Veil in Arabia: Women in Oman*. Baltimore and London: Johns Hopkins University Press.

Willan, Thomas Stuart. 1980. *Elizabethan Manchester*. Manchester: Manchester University Press for the Chetham Society.

Williams, S. K. 1978. *Rural Development in Nigeria*. Ile-Ife: University of Ife Press.

Wittmer, Charles, ed. 1946. *L'Obituaire des dominicaines d'Unterlinden*. Strasbourg and Zürich: Société Savante d'Alsace.

Wolf, Margery. 1972. *Women and the Family in Rural Taiwan*. Stanford, Calif.: Stanford University Press.

Wood, L. J. 1974. *Market Origins and Development in East Africa*. Kampala: Department of Geography, Makerere University.

World Bank. 1989. *Kenya: The Role of Women in Economic Development*. Washington, D.C.: World Bank.

World Bank. 1990. *Bangladesh: Strategies for Enhancing the Role of Women in Economic Development*. Washington, D.C.: World Bank.

Wright, Sue. 1985. "'Churmaids, Huswyfes and Hucksters': The Employment of Women in Tudor and Stuart Salisbury," in *Women and Work in Pre-Industrial England*, ed. Lindsey Charles and Lorna Duffin. London: Croom Helm. Pp. 100–121.

Wrightson, Keith, and David Levine. 1979. *Poverty and Piety in an English Village: Terling, 1525–1700*. New York: Academic Press.

Yang, Ching-Kun. 1944. *A North China Local Market Economy*. New York: Institute of Pacific Relations.

Young, Kate, ed. 1988. *Women and Economic Development: Local, Regional and National Planning Strategies*. Oxford: UNESCO.

Youssef, Nadia, and Carol Hetler. 1983. "Establishing the Economic Condition of Women-Headed Households in the Third World: A New Approach," in *Women and Poverty in the Third World*, ed. Mayra Buvinić et al. Baltimore and London: Johns Hopkins University Press. Pp. 216–43.

Zenner, Walter. 1991. *Minorities in the Middle: A Cross-Cultural Analysis*. Albany: State University of New York Press.

Index

This book has been set in Linotron Galliard. Galliard was designed for Mergenthaler in 1978 by Matthew Carter. Galliard retains many of the features of a sixteenth-century typeface cut by Robert Granjon but has some modifications that give it a more contemporary look.

Printed on acid-free paper.